Letters to a Skeptic

Ronne Gleason

Goose River Press
Waldoboro, Maine

Copyright © 2025 Ronne Gleason

All rights reserved. No part of this book may be reproduced in any form without written permission from the publisher, except by a reviewer who may quote brief passages in a review to be printed in a newspaper or magazine.

Library of Congress Card Number: 2024936657

ISBN: 978-1-59713-272-5

First Printing, 2025

Published by
Goose River Press
3400 Friendship Road
Waldoboro ME 04572
e-mail: gooseriverpress@gmail.com
www.gooseriverpress.com

A page-by-page detailed Table of Contents replaces a traditional chapter-by-chapter guide to the body of the letter.

Table of Contents

Acknowledgements vii
Introduction .... viii–x
Dedication xi
1. Jesus Stories 1
2. Imagination as a Gift 1
    A. Sufi Mysticism 2
    B. Aesop's Fables 2
    C. Adi Granth 2
    D. Iliad 2
    E. Odyssey 2
3. Shakespeare and Imagination's vulnerability 3
4. Prominent authors and their imaginations 4
5. Pessimism as a world view 4
    A. Metanoia (change) 5
6. Johannes Kepler and his religion 6
    A. Sun as a celestial Body 7
7. Karl Marx-Religion as an opiate 8
    A. Is there strength in feeling your weakness? 8
8. Plato and Aristotle on Jesus Stories 10
    A. Heidegger, Dasein and Truth Speak 10
9. Some Church History 11–13
10. Apollonius of Tyana [bi-locate] 14
11. Lost Books of the Bible 14
12. Lost Gospel According to Peter 14–15
13. Aquarian Gospel 16–19
14. Alexandria is where Jesus and David attended a Lecture of Plato 20
15. Source of Universe's Reality 20
16. Machiventa Melchizedek 20, 24–25
17. Mithras Teaching resembles Christianity 26

Table of Contents

18. Gnostic Tradition 27
19. Plato's vision of Er's resurrection 28–29
20. The Mystical Vision of the Seven Churches (Chakras)............30–32
21. Genesis Eden and Symbolic Marking(s) 33
22. Plato's Doctrine of the Cross..35–37
23. Eternal Recurrence..37
24. Science and Religion Debate...38
       A. Twain, Hume, Philo, Plato..39–46
25. Eastern Christian Orthodox Father's revered by Nietzsche 47–57
       A. Faust and Mephistophelian Zeal..57
       B. Nietzsche's eventual emotional Tumult................................58
26. Human Demands of True Faith 59
       A. The Ascetic Ideal 59
       B. Dostoevsky, and Tolstoy and Freedom in Eastern Christian Orthodoxy 60
27. Nietzsche and the Dionysian Ideal 61
28. The Holy Trinity has a numeric 777 value 62
       A. Book of Revelations and 666 ascribed to Nero.................62
       B. A possible Antichrist figure 62
29. Orphic Mysteries...64
       A. Herodotus and Pindar claimed Orpheus was an actual person..66
       B. Dionysos, Soul of the Sun 67–68
30. Thus Spake Zarathustra 67
       A. More Orphism: Did it borrow from Christianity?.............68
       B. Nietzsche's origin of Law Eternal Recurrence..................69
       C. Nietzsche and Ariadne (utterly pure female).....................69
       D. Does image of Ariadne inspire Nietzsche's ascetic ideal postulate? 69–72

Table of Contents

    E. Nietzsche's more elaborate view on exterminating the passions (The Ascetic Ideal?)..................72–74
31. John Cassian (Founder of two Monasteries) Exhorts value of Stilling desires of the Flesh..................73–74
32. Nietzsche's response to Jesus' death..................78–79
    A. Ariadne plus Dionysos unite in mystical marriage.....77–79
33. More on Dionysian Story..................78–83
34. Negative Theology and Eastern Christian Orthodoxy..............84–85
35. Nietzsche: God is Dead..................85
    A. The complex meaning of this Phrase..................85–86
36. Ubermesch or Superman and Jesus..................86
37. A rare Galactic alignment bringing the solstice sun into alignment with The Milky Way resulting in enhanced receptivity of the Chakras..................87–88
38. The Galactic inverted Tree of Life..................88
    A. The Galactic and the Crown Chakra..................88
    B. The Soul's exit from the body via crown chakra (head)...88
    C. Pythagoras required his students to eat only plant based diet, not including beans, to avoid filling top of the head (Crown Chakra) with heavy foods to keep head more buoyant.........89
39. More on Foods..................89
    A. Veneration of cows..................89–90
    B. The Eagle, and spiritualizing of material substances........91
    C. The Lion -the Sun animal..................92
    D. Butterflies..................92
40. Frances Bacon and Belief in God..................93–94
    A. Darwin's evolutionary theory (Tree of Life)..................95
    B. Sean Carroll questions the accuracy of Molecular Systematic and thus evolution..................95–96

Table of Contents

41. St. Thomas Aquinas and Immanuel Kant prove the existence of God. 96
Index..99–104
Bibliography...105–106
About the Author...107

Acknowledgements

I would Like to thank "Jerry" (actual person, but fictional name to maintain privacy) for being the sole inspiration for this long letter in response to his questions related to philosophy, religion and literature.

Also, I wish to thank Donald MacDonald, Jr. for typing from my hand written pages the Table of Contents and Index pages.

I would like to thank Professor Phillip Cary for his insights on Nietzsche, Professor Stephen Railton for his research on Mark Twain, and Professor Dennis Dalton for his research on Galileo, Newton and Johannes Kepler. Their insights added depth to my overall thesis.

LETTERS TO A SKEPTIC
(Ancients, Moderns Chime In: God is Alive)
Volume One

Introduction

My life long friend, Jerry-fictional name to retain privacy, and I debated religion, philosophy and ancient literature since the sixties, albeit during our early college days, neither one of us changing our philosophical positions very much, he the perennial skeptic, atheist even, and I the perennial believer in a master God that created and rules the universe.

For Jerry, religion is first and foremost just an opiate, a psychological palliative to help people endure their day to day sufferings. Of course, this is Karl Marx's position that he agreed with.

The above notwithstanding, Jerry would ask me poignant intellectual questions addressing specific philosophical and religious issues, asking for my opinion. Duly inspired to accommodate questions that were front and center in my religious and philosophical wheelhouse, I gladly, with intellectual fervor, responded to the questions anchoring the thrust of my arguments in my belief in God and all of the religious, philosophical and literary figures we have debated over the decades.

Now, assuming my friend did indeed respect these intellectual giants of history (he is very intelligent, not just well read), I always used these icons of thought as my source to press home my point(s) of view that always boasted of God as my premise, even mentioning such science heavy weights as Kepler, Galileo, Newton as believers in God!

I certainly did not stop there in referencing such icons in the world of science, consider, I added other notable authors to my list, for example, David Hume, Mark Twain, Immanuel Kant, Blaise Pascal, Jacob Boehme, Leo Tolstoy, The Venerable Bede, St. Augustine, Tertullian, Bacon, Taoism, Melchizedek and Plato's Doctrine of the Cross as told by Justin Martyr, to name but a few.

Knowing Jerry was not privy to a rational inductive or deductive reasoning approach to convince him of the reality of God, I instinctively knew that if I was ever to alter his skeptical position, I would have to expose him to, perhaps even for the first time, the God leaning tendencies of aforementioned iconic figures of history, a world very familiar to him.

Due to the quixotic nature of his questions, I was moved to dive deeply into any topic related to the question, exploring such esoteric subjects as Galactic Alignment Theory and its connection to man and his/her chakras (powerful wheels of energy situated along the spine), Rudolph Steiner's views on Man's spiritual relationship to the cow, eagle, lion, and butterfly, and a lengthy exploration of the virtues of Active Imagination, along with many more ancillary subjects that helped drive home my point that an All Seeing God does indeed exist.

It is my sincere hope that the reader not just gain knowledge of philosophy, literature and religion in general, but will want to study further the icons of history referred to in this letter.

Picture of author's
parents drawing in
graphite 11 x 17
Titled: Mom & Dad
1995
By Ronne Gleason

Bust photo of my dad.
In jest, my dad
referred to himself as
the "Great One"
(1915–1999). My dad
posed six months for
this bust, and I completed it two weeks
before his passing.
Thank God!
Ronne Gleason

Dedication

I would like to dedicate this book to my parents who enjoyed a 50 year exemplary marriage of whom my brother and I are the blessed result.

Letters to a Skeptic

Dear Jerry,

Received your letter today and will respond immediately so you can receive it ahead of your departure to Arizona.

The allegation that the stories of Jesus could have been relegated to mere sophistry violates the purpose of the stories (see my excerpt of Josephus's testimonies enclosed) which is to embrace truth, an ideal anathema to sophistry which is to win an argument irrespective of truth as I alluded to in my latest letter. Plato and Aristotle were both truth seekers, a matter of life or death for them; a stance they learned well from Socrates. More on this later.

Your negative tone regarding imagination incited by the Jesus stories implies you lack formal knowledge/study on the great gift imagination affords. If you reread my Emerson essay you will note that in addition to personal revelation, imagination is central to elevating consciousness. Moreover, he acquired the idea of the significance of the imagination from Jacob Boehme, a prominent Christian esotericist. Boehme studied Hermes who proclaimed the necessity for imagination. Islamic mystics also proclaim the necessity for imagination to elevate consciousness. Jerry, I do not wish to expand too much on this because to do the subject justice it would take too much time. However, my Emerson essay is a good starting point. Yes, indeed, imagination goes all the way back to Egypt (Hermes), a history you have already indicated an interest in.

Additionally, since we are created in God's image (maybe implausible to you), and God's Imagination created the worlds, and every moment recreates these worlds in the Human being in whom He has revealed His perfect image according to Islamic mysticism, we likewise, via our Active Imagination, are inherently capable of doing the same. That is, engage our imagination which is Recurrent, just as, and because, the Creation is Recurrent. This is why, according to Sufi mysticism, man's Active Imagination cannot be vain fiction as found in some of Shakespeare's characters, especially Macbeth, since it is the same theophanic (a manifestation or appearance of God, or a god to man) Imagination which, in and by the individual, continues to reveal what it showed itself by first imagining it. This very imagination can only be termed illusory when it becomes opaque (impenetrable to infusion of light-a weighted Zoharic theme), and loses its transparency. Mystic perception is transparent, and thus melds the seeming gap between God and Man by bridging this same gap with the enhanced perception of Active Imagination.

Well, just as *Aesop's Fables* served as inspired reading material for Socrates, feeding his Active Imagination with prolific insights (I'm assuming this based upon his reported dedication to their study), I can only surmise that Plato and Aristotle embraced the same study. It's common knowledge that Plato chose dialogue to be the most effective way to teach his ideas; the Sufis, most notably Rumi, among several others, chose short stories to teach their truths. So, even if they considered the Jesus stories mere fables, they would have, just as Socrates embraced *Aesop's Fables*, very likely have read them with zeal for learning purposes. Moreover, the study of scripture, whether it be the *Koran, Bhagavad-Gita*, Christian and Hebrew bibles, *Adi Granth, Iliad* or *The Odyssey* and the like, all serve to invoke Active Imagination, inspire brand new perceptions or epiphanies as it very famously did with St. Augustine of Hippo. There are documented cases where readers of the *Koran*, upon the very first reading, could memorize the entire text. The Hebrew scriptures, according to Rabbinic scholars, have a similar effect and more, due to the especial design of their alphabet and numeric intimations. I expound this very important Hebraic topic in my doctoral thesis, *Can Man Influence God*. My study of the Koran over the years has been profoundly inspirational, probably aided by the fact that it is the only complete scripture (arguably or unarguably, I'm not sure) that came directly from God to a single individual.

While only a moderate study of Shakespeare can reveal that the imagination is vulnerable to irrational influences creating in the person a melange of conflicting forces, the source of which is unclear (Shakespeare is well known for his adoration of abnormal states of mind), the chances of being likewise influenced by the study of Jesus' stories are quite remote, but, like anything, not impossible, after all, said stories are potent; in fact so powerful, according to the Christian and all religious traditions, that scriptures are intentionally woven around parables and riddles, and arguably, intentional contradictions/discrepancies to prevent the Unprepared from acquiring a higher knowledge they are not ready for.

Look at the positive effect scripture study (Jesus stories suited for the scrap heap as you stated in your letter) had on Tolstoy. He began a life of charitable giving, embraced a relatively abstemious lifestyle, halted all hunting, even embracing vegetarianism in 1884, concluding that he must repent, live self-sufficiently, live and eat simply (a far cry from his usual gourmet foods) and engage in manual labor. Tolstoy surmised manual labor reduced sexual desire in addition to simply humbling him. He embraced this lifestyle change during the last three decades of his life amid his conversion to Christianity. Note: I typed in last few years in my last letter by mistake-unintentionally. I never proofed it. Finally, Tolstoy's new vision can be seen by his words direct: "We can understand the existence of God only when we feel our complete dependence on him, just like an infant feels when his mother holds him. A baby does not know who feeds him, who warms him, who takes care of him, but he understands that there is someone who does this, and thus loves the force in whose power he rests" (*Spiritual Writings*, 176). In this same volume Tolstoy informs of his affinity for Blaise Pascal's proclamation about man: "There are only three kinds of people: first, those who find God and serve him; secondly, those who, not finding him, are occupied in the search for him; and thirdly, those who neither find him nor seek him. The first are **reasonable** and happy; the last are unreasonable and unhappy; those in between are unhappy but reasonable" (175). My emphasis on Tolstoy is due to a statement you made several months ago in response to my mentioning some of his quotes indicating his allegiance to Christ. You said that it was probably some mis-translation and not from him direct. That is why I provided you with the numerous excerpts in the last letter to demonstrate Tolstoy's own words which inform of his powerful allegiance to Christ. I find it curious that you never iterated his conversion to Christ, and even if you don't like his ideas about his Christian alliance, when speaking of him, you should have mentioned your awareness of Tolstoy the new man, since the old man, the man of his novels is no more, at least that's how he wants his readers of his later writings to perceive him. This is very typical of any religious conversion, an experience you do not have any intimate connection to, so you naturally downplay it, when in fact, it is a very big event in a person's life. If only Maupassant and Chekhov, noted pessimists, could have experienced the same awakening, and whether adventitious or gradual through basic life experiences that echoed the Solomon-like theme that all is vanity/futile to the core, they may have altered their affinity for weaving their stories (Maupassant) and plays and stories (Chekhov) around the common folk, i.e. the tragedy that eternally lurks in the commonplace. Consider, even Maupassant's story *Happiness*, after surrounding a drab situation that elicits one's sympathy for two old people, accentuates the cruelty and bitterness of human life. He is a genius tale teller indeed. But unlike Tolstoy, according to my reading, he never transcended his bleak outlook on life. As I implied earlier, man needs to overcome himself to be in this world joyfully, and not really of it (a common Sufi theme and Christian ideal). Chesterton says of Tolstoy, and perhaps he would have likewise opined about Chekhov and Maupassant, that Tolstoy "went mad because he was not a mystic." In other words, his imagination was too opaque, less so after his conversion however. Chesterton, like C. S. Lewis, converted to Christian Orthodoxy, I believe later in life. Chesterton's book *Orthodoxy* is a masterpiece. Chesterton died twenty-six years after Tolstoy.

To view the world through pessimistic eyes, wherein one will only end up in oblivion upon translation (death to physical body), as you implied, has a way of inadvertently abrogating one from accepting personal responsibility to perfect oneself, to sacrifice oneself for an ideal greater than oneself. "Christ did not tell us to love one another, but preached repentance, *metanoia*, that is to say, a change of thinking regarding life itself: change your whole conception of life, He said, or you will perish" (*Spiritual Writings*, Leo Tolstoy, 202). "...The main thing is that I am preparing for death, i.e., for another life, and this preparation consists entirely in living as well as possible and trying to understand what can be understood. I believe that all this will be useful *there*, as it is here" (201). In these lines Tolstoy captures poignant Gurdjieffian themes.

Jerry, if scientific giants such as Isaac Newton and Galileo Galilei (coincidently dying the day Newton was born) did not believe the Jesus stories were mere sophistry why would Plato and Aristotle? All four had enormous **imaginations** hence their scientific gifts to the outer world. Attesting to Newton's religious faith, consider the following excerpt taken from a manuscript now in the Jewish National and University Library in Jerusalem (*Yehuda Ms.* 15.3, fol 46r):

...For though there be that are called God whether in Heaven or in [on] earth (as there are gods many and lords many) yet to us there is but one God the father of whom are all things and we in him and one Lord Jesus Christ by whom are all things and we by him: that is, but one God and one Lord in our worship.

For Galileo we learn of his allegiance to the church: "...first that in my writings cannot be found the faintest shadow of irreverence to the Holy Church [not my caps]; and second, the testimony of my own conscience, which only I and God in Heaven thoroughly know. And he knows that in this cause for which I suffer (he confirmed the Copernican opinion in his *Dialogue on the Two Great World Systems*, thus violating the Church's instructions), though many might have spoken with more learning, none, not even the ancient Fathers, have spoken with more piety or greater zeal for the Church than I."

Also, I might add, that Johannes Kepler took his religion very seriously, and while he was expelled from his home for refusing to embrace Roman Catholicism and the Lutheran doctrine, he was suspected of being a secret Calvinist even though he objected to Calvin's doctrine of predestination. In short, he did affirm, "In general I do not favor any teaching which cannot be found in the old Fathers of the Church." Kepler stated that when the Bible refers to natural objects and events, it should not be taken literally. While Kepler did believe that the Bible should be interpreted rationally, he did embrace the various Christian mysteries such as the Holy Trinity and the Incarnation. By the way, he also believed intuitively that the sun was a celestial body, in fact, the home of Jesus Christ. Yes, he was accused of sun worship. Recall my earlier letter extolling the sun's significance in cosmology and in George Gurdjieff's teachings.

In deference to your expressed regard for Egyptian study, and also my recent reference to the sun in Gurdjieff's cosmology, and of course, aforementioned prominent scientist, Johannes Kepler's obvious affinity for the sun, and a possible inspiration for his belief, consider one poignant Egyptian Oracle:

> Above the Celestial Fire there is an Incorruptible Flame, ever sparkling, Source of Life, Fountain of all Beings, and Principle of all Things...It girdles the Heavens and from it there proceeds a tiny spark which makes the whole fire of the Sun, Moon and Stars. This is what I know of God. Seek not to know more, for this passes thy comprehension however so wise thou mayest be. Nevertheless, know that the unjust and wicked man cannot hide himself from God, nor can craft nor excuse disguise aught from His piercing eyes. All is full of God, God is everywhere.

I should note here that notable skeptic Montaigne, in culling his opinion from Cicero, said that Oracles had diminished their learning aid, or efficacy over time.

Jerry, I only reference these scientists of old because you frequently emphasize your need to see religion through scientific eyes as though a person who is scientific wouldn't be religious or believe in such irrational things as Christianity. Frankly, I think you are in small company.

You should know that I have been studying science for three decades starting from occult chemistry, projective geometry, physics, cosmology, and now string theory. If anything, as some modern day physicists proclaim, one's belief in the Christian mysteries is enhanced, and if not enhanced, then at least not diminished through scientific studies. I'm not going to cite sources for this last statement because it is not that important to my prevailing discussion.

Now, your attachment of imagination to a need for emotional security "(believe and you will live forever)" suggests a certain naivete about all spiritual teachings through the ages, and an unwitting or intentional reference to Marx's opinion that religion is merely an "opiate for the masses;" an age old assertion commonly known. I use the term spiritual naivete because Taoism, Christianity, Hinduism, Sikhism, Buddhism and Islamism all demand that their followers recognize their own weakness, their own sickness, their nothingness, in order to sacrifice their bloated selves for something greater than themselves, as in, e.g., "deny yourselves and follow me." This adroitly alleges to the wisdom found in insecurity, in recognizing one's own insecurity inadvertently seeking to gain strength from this wisely acknowledged personal weakness through a force greater than themselves. Most call it God. As Paul says, you are made strong in your weakness by relying on your Creator. For those inclined toward atheism, many will feel their own greatness/that is, their own something-ness-a common view, and Imagine they can rely on themselves for achieving a greater sense of purpose in life. The former realizations are humbling, and frankly, foolish from the point of view of the world. The world is smothered in worldly cleverness, and for one to be a fool of God is anathema to being a wise guy in the world. By making a choice to be a fool of God for reasons of personal revelation, personal suffering and the like, one can find comfort in a supersensual/natural God, thus obliging His calling and no creature can judge the efficacy or non-efficacy of this (beyond words) experience. Because you seem to respect the Greek tradition, consider these two poignant Greek proverbs: "The poor have not, but God has," as in, says Paul the Apostle, "Blessed are the poor in spirit (realize one's lowliness) for theirs is the kingdom of heaven;"(MT 5:3); Or, another Greek Proverb, "One thing I know, is that I know nothing." And furthermore, because this absurd allegiance requires an unrequited faith, note this third poignant Greek proverb, "Faith is the power of life." And, in these purported realizations the seed is now planted, wherein one can pay back existence/God for the occasion of their life. Jerry, you seem prone to judge these matters as mere folly, and your limited personal experience does not give you the intellectual ammunition to make astute assessments. After all, it does not appear to me that you have ever had a personal supernatural revelation, an experience that cannot be had through intellectual pondering. Just my guess, only you can know.

About a year ago I read in one of my science journals that a cardiologist is on a mission to prove the realness of out of body experiences. So far he has collected thirteen experiences/cases from people who had cardiac arrests and came back to life. (Recall that my uncle had an out of body experience that I already told you about.) The details are vague, but I think his hope was/is to uncover a method to reduce the harmful after-effects like memory loss created from the heart stopping.

All these traditions require the need to still the thoughts, or bare the attention, DISIDENTIFY with one's own opinions; that is, metaphorically chop one's head off, a head that is simply full of so much mental stuff and intellectual vigor, it creates a road block to elevated consciousness, a consciousness that moves out in front of the body initially, and then, finally out. As Paul says, "you are not your body," or "out of body or no."

Jerry, I rarely, if ever, hear you speak, or inquire about matters of self identification, attention and the like. The idea of collecting attention (being in the waking state) successfully is a life long endeavor, and I really do not believe you see the importance of this pursuit, and actually is the most critical message of all religions for at least one major reason: one cannot pray successfully, or focus on God, unless one can do so without experiencing invading THOUGHTS that forever divert one's attention, an attention completely alien to one's effort.

Ronne Gleason

One more thought on Plato and Aristotle regarding your comment about the Jesus stories as being mere sophistry. While it's not possible to comment adroitly on either person since they lived before Jesus, consider that Heidegger stated in his book, *Plato's Sophist*, that humanity has been without a discussion of Dasein (being-being-ness-consciousness-being awake) for twenty-five hundred years, asserting that this crucial topic has been covered over by so much idle talk, it leads to untruth through the centuries. Adding that opinions rigidify themselves in concepts and propositions that become truisms repeated over and over, with the consequence that what was originally disclosed becomes covered over/up again. Thus everyday Dasein suffers a double cover-up, and it is/was the "Intention of the spiritual writings of Socrates, Plato and Aristotle to battle against this idle talk. Their struggle against rhetoric and sophistry bears witness to it" (p. 11). By the way, this same thing is what Gurdjieff is about. He never allowed his followers to ask questions about philosophy and the like because they only filled the head with more rubbish to get rid of. Only personal questions (nothing intellectual) were permitted. Okay, now considering Heidegger's assessment of Plato and Aristotle and their penchant for truth seek, and the stories of Jesus, at the very least, teaching stories as some scholars proclaim, then I'd guess that they would approve of them, since they were ardent truth seekers-Know thyself (being-ness) as were all the individual religious leaders who knew of them, including even Mohammed.

Some thoughts to consider on your allegation of conflicting accounts in church history. First, no educated person would dispute this allegation due to the very nature of its source accumulation. The written sources include official documents of ecclesiastical and civil authorities: acts of councils and synods, confessions of faith, letters of popes and bishops; Private writings of personal actors in history: works of church fathers, heretics and heathen authors for the first six centuries; of the missionaries, scholastic and mystic divines for the middle ages; and of the reformers and their opponents, for the sixteenth century. Note that these writings must be carefully sifted, especially the controversial ones. Next are the accounts of chroniclers and historians, whether friends or enemies, who were eyewitnesses to what they relate, each also to be carefully considered. These documents were wholly or partially lost, like many of Eusebius' authorities for the period before Constantine, or are inaccessible to historians, as are the papal regesta and other documents of the Vatican library. (At this point see my two pages excerpted from *The First Christian Histories*). Next are inscriptions on tombs revealing the faith and hope of Christians in times of persecution. I recall Tertullian (a very prominent and influential African Church Father-c.160-c.225) saying that there is more history on the blood of one's tomb than in anything one writes. This is the approximate wording (very close though) in response to your assertion about death occurring amongst those who professed any contrary religion. And also, more history can be found among the ruins of Egypt and Babylonia where complete libraries have been disentombed and deciphered containing mythological and religious records, astronomical and poetic expositions that revealed an extinct civilization shedding some light on the Old Testament history. These are the written sources.

The unwritten sources are church paintings and sculpture, religious customs and ceremonies which were very important for the history of worship and ecclesiastical art connoting a significance for the spirit of the age. I suggest you read Bedes' very thorough book, *Ecclesiastical Histories*. I had to read this book for one of my Harvard seminars. These works of art were/are symbolical representations of the various types of Christianity. In this regard, John Singer Sargent's massive religious murals painted on the walls of the Boston Public Library boasted the following titles: *Triumph of Religion, illustrating certain stages of Jewish and Christian history, The Frieze of the Prophets, Dogma of the Redemption, Frieze of the*

Ronne Gleason

Angels, Crucifix, Handmaid of the Lord, Madonna of Sorrows, The Fifteen Mysteries or the Meditation of the Rosary, Fall of Gog and Magog, Messianic Era, personified representations of *Synagogue and Church*, and *Judgment*, accompanied by illustrations of *Hell and Heaven*.

While Sargent was not committed to any religion, he did subscribe to it nevertheless. He placed a high value on the symbolic and aesthetic aspect of religion labeling him an exoticist, wherein he downplayed a personal faith in the paintings, but amplified its identity with primitive and elemental feelings accompanied by elevated thoughts and values. Even though the Boston Public Library is not a church, Sargent made it seem like one with especial Christian and Jewish messages painted throughout its halls and ceilings. A foreign visitor, not otherwise familiar with Christianity, could, as result of Sargent's works, obtain a fair idea of its teachings, that is, its historical genesis.

The three periods of history are as follows: History of Ancient Christianity from birth of Christ to Gregory the Great, A.D. 1-590. Medieval Christianity, from Gregory I to the reformation, A.D. 590-1517. However, this middle age is often seen from Constantine, 306 or 311; from the fall of west Roman Empire, 476; from Gregory the Great, 590; and from Charlemagne, 800. But it generally is regarded as closing at the beginning of the sixteenth century, even more precisely, at the outbreak of the Reformation in 1517. The third period is Modern Christianity, from the reformation to the present time, A.D. 1517-1880 (*History of the Christian Church*, Phillip Schaff, vol. 1,11-17).

The above history provides the historical approach to church history, leaving the religious approach open for investigation of which I will not detail. However, consider that scholars do say that the Gospels contain stories that are trying to convey truths about Jesus, but are not historically accurate, at least not historically accurate as they are narrated. A further note on the difference in the way

Jesus is portrayed between *Mark, Luke* and *John*. In *Mark*, Jesus is not divine, but clearly God's favored one; In Luke, Jesus seems to be seen as divine whose father is not a mortal but God Himself (1:35). In Mark, the assumption seems that Joseph is Jesus' father with no account of his virgin birth. (One scholar wrote that portions of *Mark* are modeled after Homer's *Odyssey*). In *John*, Jesus is equal to God, but this is not the same as saying that he was identical with God. Later Christians however, made this claim, leading, in the fourth century, to the formulation of the Nicene Creed, in which Jesus is affirmed as being fully divine and fully human simultaneously. The story of Jesus is extensive Jerry, but I wanted to provide you with my brief take to respond to your concerns about the discrepancies in Christian history that are well known among all seminarians and priests, and of course, church scholars, but that does not take away from the Belief factored into this very enormous enigma called Christianity. Recall, that I mentioned in my last letter that Jesus, like Allah, like Buddha, like Krishna are individuals'/Gods of Belief. Noteworthy, is that, as of the year two thousand, there were two thousand and forty-five books and articles about Jesus that represented radically different conclusions. And this does not even include my esoteric intimations of Jesus (a bit more on this later). Continuing briefly on the cycle of exoteric historicity, Pliny the Younger and Tacitus offer some brief information on Jesus. And the first century Palestinian historian Flavius Josephus (see enclosed excerpt taken from my 938 page book, *The Works of Josephus*) provides a little more data, much more than my one page excerpt reveals.

As you peruse my variegated source rendering, can you not imagine how all sorts of conclusions can be arrived at, and your referenced Einhorn "hypothesis" is just one among thousands. My Phillip Schaff set is eight volumes totaling approximately eight thousand pages of Christian History, but of course, it is not as up to date as Einhorn's as though that is supposed to matter.

Ronne Gleason

Interestingly, I think it is interesting anyway, that the Bible of Greek culture is Homer's *Iliad* and *Odyssey*, and yet scholars do not know for sure if their ever was a person named Homer. Like the Christian Bible, it could have been composed by several writers. In fact, there is even doubt if the battle of Troy ever occurred. During my early conversion days I even pondered if Apollonius of Tyana, a contemporary of Jesus, though they never knew each other, was as divine as Jesus. After all, their followers would argue who was superior, Jesus or Apollonius of Tyana, whom could also bi-locate (be in two places at the same time). The same anomaly could be said about Shakespeare. Was Christopher Marlowe, Cervantes or Bacon the real Shakespeare, and/or were the plays simply written by several writers?! Twain insisted Shakespeare never wrote a single play.

Now, acknowledge that the above historical assessments, though not conclusive, are canonical in purpose. I have always had a strong interest in the non-canonical, more esoteric, even occult approach to Christian history. And without going into much detail, way too huge a subject, especially after four decades of personal study in this particular area, consider studying the book, *The Lost Books of the Bible*, translated from the original tongues with a foreword by Solomon J. Schepps. The documents written in this book came soon after Christ's resurrection. In regard to your concern about the first 350 years after the birth of Jesus, the books in this collection were suppressed by the church at the end of the fourth century when the Bible was finally compiled. So reading these poignant documents should prove valuable to your investigation as they have for me over the decades, not to mention the inspiration they provided. One important text is the *Lost Gospel According to Peter*, that boasts twenty-nine variations of fact between this lost gospel and the four canonical gospels. On numerous occasions this lost gospel was referred to by several Fathers of the orthodox church. It was first referred to by Serapion, Bishop of Antioch, in

190 A.D., and rediscovered by the French Archaeological Mission at Cairo, in 1886, while excavating in the grave of a monk, the name of whom I do not know.

I said earlier that the Jesus stories are enigmatic, often purely allegorical, which Jesus says he will explain later but rarely does. Moreover, amid his persistent attestation to be the great revealer of truth, he continues to veil his message. He does this because the Jesus story is part of the Outer Mysteries of Christianity, designed for psychic initiates, that is, the active and contemplative initiates who embrace good works of which Mary and Martha are prime examples. On the other hand, the secret teachings of the resurrected Christ (by the way, in *The Lost Gospel According to Peter*, the resurrection and the Ascension occur on the same day), are designed to teach initiates in the pneumatic state, that is, a state where the initiate is presumed capable of a philosophical understanding of the Inner Mysteries leading to passive witnessing. These Inner Mysteries are found in certain Gnostic gospels, for example, *The Pistis Sophia,* a third century Egyptian work which purports to provide Jesus' teachings to certain disciples at the end of his twelve year sojourn on earth after the resurrection. It relates the salvation of the personified *Pistis Sophia* (i.e. faith-wisdom) from a demon named self-will. The *Gnostic* gospels, like Eastern Orthodoxy, are woven around ascetic practices, i.e. annihilation of self-will. Additional Gnostic gospels are *The Book of Leou, The Book of the Great Logos, According to the Mystery and the Book of the Saviour*. For Gnostics, like Jesus and premier Neo-Platonist, Plotinus, the core teaching is God is Love. You could say that the Jesus myth, as some would infer, is a simple initiation allegory; And just as Paul was not concerned with the historical man in Jesus, but rather the Mystical Christ in us, so should we be likewise absorbed. Jerry, recall I have indicated to you several times that, while Roman Catholicism is concerned predominantly with scholasticism in its Christian teaching, which is fine, not entirely anathema to

Orthodoxy, Eastern Orthodoxy is the Mystical tradition, the mystical spoke on the wheel of Christianity, the original Christianity. Not far askance, actually right on, from this purport of the Mystical Christ within, is a statement by St. Augustine of Hippo, in his *Retractions* that reads as follows:

> That which is called the Christian religion existed among the ancients, and never did not exist, from the beginnings of the human race until Christ came in the flesh, at which time the true religion, which already existed, began to be called Christianity (1.13.3).

We are now standing upon the cusp of the Piscean-Aquarian Ages. Fish was a Christian symbol, esoterically and exoterically. The former see fish as being symbolic of the sperm, and exoterically, a fish is sculpted on numerous Christian monuments, and more particularly, upon the ancient sarcophagi. It is also upon medals bearing the name of Jesus, and also upon engraved stones. Baptismal fonts are ornamented with the fish.

In the writings of church father, Tertullian, we find his words: "We are little fishes in Christ our great fish.?"

Let the above comments serve as my preface to the *Aquarian* [spiritual] *Gospel of Jesus The Christ*. Within the 260 pages of this work are numerous teachings of Jesus direct. This point notwithstanding, I mention this to you only in lieu of your interest expressed in your letter regarding the years prior to 350 A.D., that have been deleted, actually, never recognized, by the Nicene Creed.

In these writings you will find the following chapters, among many others, in verse: Life and Works of Jesus in India, Life and Works of Jesus in Persia, Life and Works of Jesus in Egypt, Life and Works of Jesus in Greece, Life and Works of Jesus in Assyria, Life and Works of Jesus in Tibet and Western India. These make for very provocative stories and were the sole inspiration of one man, referred to as Levi.

When Jesus was in Egypt he attended the sacred school of Elihu and Salome in Zoan where he earned the following degrees: first degree in Sincerity; second degree Justice; third degree in Faith; Fourth degree in Philanthropy; fifth degree Heroism; sixth degree in Love Divine; and the highest, or seventh degree (there is that reference to the all significant law of seven-Octaves that rules the planet), The Christ. While this Gospel does not provide the precise date, it was stated in chapter 55:9, "Go on your way, for you must/preach the gospel of good will to men/ and peace on earth; must open/up the prison doors and set the captives free" [last line is vague]. Forward to verse 10, we read: "And while the hierophant [Jesus became a private pupil of the hierophant-an interpreter of sacred mysteries or esoteric principles] yet spoke/ the temple bells rang out;/ a pure white dove descended from above/and sat on Jesus' head. Verse 11: "And then a voice that shook/ the very temple said, This is the Christ/ and every living creature said,/AMEN, verse 12: "The great doors of the temple/swung ajar; the logos journeyed [Egypt was Jesus' last visit to a sacred school] on his way a conqueror."

From the perspective of Christian scholarship, we must consider that the first fifty years of the Christian era is riddled in numerous misapprehensions, and therefore, the above *Aquarian Gospel* would be subject to considerable dispute as to its authenticity. Yet, the existence of Christianity in Egypt so soon after the supposed date of the crucifixion is also attested to in an account by Josephus, a prominent Christian historian I already mentioned. Josephus records that in the A.D. 50s a missionary from Egypt (Jesus) appeared in Jerusalem itself (in 55:3 of the *Aquarian Gospel*, the hierophant proclaims upon Jesus earning his seventh degree, The Christ, "This is the royal day for all the hosts of Israel....") where he is said to have had greater success than John the Baptist, as he gathered 30,000 Jews under his leadership. The newcomer (Jesus) said "he was a prophet, and advised the multitude of the common people to go along with him to the Mount of Olives...He said further that he would show them from thence how, at His command, the walls of Jerusalem would fall down...Now when Felix [the Roman procurator] was informed of these things he ordered his soldiers to take their weapons...and attacked the Egyptian [Jesus] and the people that were with him. He [Felix] slew four hundred [of the 30,000 Jews] and took two hundred alive. But the Egyptian himself escaped out of the fight...." This account by Josephus implies that the Egyptian must have been a Messianic teacher, for the Jews would not have followed him had he been a pagan prophet. Later, when Paul made his last visit to Jerusalem in A.D. 57, and had to be rescued by Roman soldiers from the wrath of the Jews, the Roman captain mistook him for the Egyptian rebel [Jesus] prophet and asked him: "Art thou that Egyptian, which before these days made an uproar, and led four thousand men who were murderers out into the wilderness." (*Christianity, An Ancient Egyptian Religion*, Ahmed Osman, 189)? Osman must have acquired this story from *Acts 21:28*.

Recall that in the *Lost Gospel According to Peter*, this precious document was found in Cairo, Egypt; well, stated in the 14th and final verse is: "But I, Simon Peter, and Andrew/my brother took our nets/ and went to the sea; and there was/ with us Levi the son of Alphaeus, whom the Lord..." And also, Levi was prophesied approximately two thousand years ago by Elihu, who conducted a school for the prophets in Zoan, Egypt, (recall this is where Jesus attended according to this account as I indicated earlier) who said this of Levi: "This age will comprehend but little of the works of Purity and Love; but not a word is lost, for in the Book of God's Remembrance [otherwise known as Akashic records], a record is made of every thought and word and deed; And when the world is ready to receive, lo, God will send a messenger to open up the book and copy from its sacred pages all the messages of Purity and

Love... And man again will be at one with God" (*Aquarian Gospel*, 7:25-28).

In Christian scholarship Levi is referred to as Levi, son of Alphaeus, the tax collector called by Christ to be one of his disciples; and according to Papias (c. 60-130), bishop of Hierapolis in Asia Minor, Levi made a collection of Christ's sayings in Hebrew, and he is traditionally held to be the author of the first gospel or *Matthew* c. A.D. 80-90. In the *Aquarian Gospel's Introduction* his life is mentioned only in brief, and is said to have received his inspiration to transcribe this *Aquarian Gospel* from his uncanny sensitivity to the finer ethers that in some way created sensitized plates on which sounds, even thoughts, were recorded that he was eventually able to pick up. With sincere devotion he entered into deeper studies of etheric vibrations, determined to solve the mysteries of the heavens. As a result of his efforts, inspiration came to him to draft the manuscript entitled "*The Cusp of the Ages*," the partial draft of which is formed as part of the introduction to *The Aquarian Gospel of Jesus the Christ*, alleging "That Jesus was man and that Christ was God, so that in every truth Jesus the Christ was the God-man of the ages" (Intro, p.9). Moreover, know that this same gospel asserts that Jesus had to work for his Christ status, i.e., witness his attendance at the aforementioned sacred schools in various countries. Now, could The Lost Gospel According to Peter be a major piece in this mysterious Jesus puzzle, that is, its mention of Levi whom could also be a pseudo name? I find the connection interesting, not to mention, the very study of both gospels, is very revealing.

On the esoteric side Levi is considered, as stated in the *Aquarian Gospel*, to be an Enoch initiate. While Enoch is an Old Testament patriarch, many legends became attached to his name. *The Book of Enoch*, or Ethiopic Enoch, so called because it survives in its most complete form in Ethiopic, is one of the most Jewish pseudepigrapha (certain writings, other than the canonical books and the apocrypha, professing to be Biblical in character, but not considered canonical or inspired).

Adding to the early years of Jesus, my Melchizedek volume provides a concise extrapolation of each year in the life of Jesus, including all his visits to foreign lands while they were en route to Rome. The main places visited were Caesarea, Alexandria, Lasea in Crete, Carthage, and Malta to not only learn, but bring truth to others. These journeys were taken with his Philistine interpreter, Gadiath, who worked for Simon the tanner, and two natives from India, Gonod and his son Ganid. They departed Jerusalem on a Sunday morning, April 26, A.D. 22. As Jesus discovered, Gadiath was a truth seeker, and they both subsequently became warm friends; and as the two India natives became increasingly aware of Jesus' unusual perception, he earned their profound admiration making for one exquisite traveling threesome.

In Alexandria, Jesus and Ganid attended a lecture on Plato at the university, wherein Jesus interpreted the meaning of the lecture to the young lad, Ganid, without injecting any teaching of his own. While Jesus approved of some of the Greek teachings that dealt with the theory that the material things of the world are shadowy reflections of the invisible, but more substantial spiritual realities, He (Jesus) wanted to lay a more trustworthy foundation on the nature of these realities so the lad could understand them. In modern phraseology this is what Jesus said to Ganid:

> The source of the universe's reality is infinite. The material things of the finite creation are the time-space repercussions of the Paradise Pattern and the Universal Mind of the eternal God. Causation in the physical world, self consciousness in the intellectual world, and progressing selfhood in the spirit world-these realities, projected on a universal scale, combined in eternal relatedness, and experienced with perfection of quality and divinity of value-constitute the reality of the Supreme. But in an ever-changing universe of the Original

Personality of causation, intelligence, and spirit, experience is changeless Absolute. All things, even in an eternal universe of limitless values and divine qualities, may, and oftentimes do, change except the Absolutes and that which has attained the physical status, intellectual embrace, or spiritual identity which is absolute.

The highest level to which a finite creature can progress is the recognition of the Universal Father and the knowing of the Supreme. And even then such beings of finality—destiny go on experiencing change in motions of the physical and its material phenomena. Likewise, do they remain in their selfhood progression in their continuing ascension of the spiritual universe and of growing consciousness in their deepening appreciation of, and response to, the intellectual cosmos. [This point echoes a very important component of the Gurdjieff teaching]. Only in the perfection, harmony, and unanimity of will can the creature become as one with the Creator; and such a state of divinity is attained and maintained only by the creature's continuing to live in time and eternity by consistently conforming his finite personal will of the Creator....

Life is an adaptation of the original cosmic causation to the demands and possibilities of universe situations, and it comes into being by the action of the Universal mind and the activation of the spirit spark of the God who is spirit. The meaning of life is its adaptability; the value of life is its progressability even to the heights of God-consciousness.

Mis-adaptation of self-conscious life to the universe results in cosmic disharmony. Final divergence of personality will, from the trend of the universes, terminate in intellectual isolation and personality segregation. Loss of the indwelling spirit pilot supervenes in spiritual cessation of the universe. Intelligent and progressive life becomes then, incontrovertible proof of the existence of a purposeful universe expressing the will of a divine Creator. [This teleological idea and intimation of man's inherent responsibility to care for the well being of the universe is Gurdjieffian, and I wonder if he could have, at least in part, derived his opinion-his teaching in this regard, from this affirmation of Jesus; this would support this very same Hindu idea that he had studied].

Error (evil) is the penalty of imperfection. The qualities of imperfection, or the facts of mis-adaptation are disclosed on the material level by critical observation and scientific analysis; on a moral level, by human experience. The presence of evil constitutes the inaccuracies of mind, and the immaturity of the evolving self. Evil is, therefore, a measure of imperfection in universe interpretation. The possibility in making mistakes is inherent in the acquisition of wisdom, the scheme of progressing from the partial and temporal to the complete and eternal, from the relative and imperfect, to final and perfected. Error is the shadow of relative incompleteness which must of necessity fall across man's ascending universe path to Paradise perfection. Error (evil) is not an actual universe quality; it is simply the observation of a relativity in the relatedness of the imperfection of incomplete finite to the ascending levels of the Supreme and Ultimate.

All static, dead concepts are potentially evil [inherent necessary incompleteness in God's revelation]. The finite shadow of relative and living truth is continuing moving. Static concepts invariably retard science, politics, society, and religion. Static concepts may represent a certain knowledge, but they are deficient in wisdom and devoid of truth. But do not permit the concept to mislead you that you fail to recognize the coordination of the universe under the guidance of the cosmic mind, and its stabilized control by the energy and spirit of the Supreme (1433-34).

Continuing their learning in Alexandria, Jesus and Ganid investigated some of the one million manuscripts in its library. Jesus, in endeavoring to point out to young Ganid the truth in each said, "But Yahweh is the God developed from the revelations of Melchizedek and the covenant of Abraham. The Jews were the offspring of Abraham, and subsequently occupied the very land wherein Melchizedek had lived and taught, and from which he sent teachers to all the world; and their religion eventually portrayed a clearer recognition of the Lord God of Israel as the Universal Father in heaven more so than any other world religion" (1432.). Ganid and Jesus spent considerable time discussing Philo, a famous religious philosopher known as the Pythagorian, who attempted to harmonize Greek philosophy and Hebrew theology. Intent on attending some of Philo's lectures while in Alexandria, Jesus and Ganid were unable to do so due to Philo's illness during their stay in Alexandria.

Ganid, in telling Jesus that he knew more than the professors they were listening to, informed Ganid, "These teachers are not minded that you and I should instruct them. The pride of un-spiritualized learning is a treacherous thing in human experience. The true teacher maintains his intellectual integrity by ever remaining a learner" (1433). At times Ganid would refer to Jesus as teacher Joshua (defined as the Lord saves, which is the Greek form of the Hebrew name). The Joshua/Jesus link first appeared in Exodus 17:9. St. Justin Martyr, (C.100-C.165), an Apologist, first accused of atheism, converted to Christianity in c.130. He taught Christianity in Ephesus and later in Rome. Justin refers to the Old Testament Joshua 38 times (I found 213 references to Joshua in O.

T.) in an effort to convince the Jew Trypho that the Hebrew scriptures are full of references to Jesus. Could a pre-Christian cult have evolved around the Joshua/Jesus story many centuries prior to the supposed birth of Christianity? In *Zechariah* 3, Joshua is invested as high priest by the "Angel of the Lord," and is later crowned as Messiah (Zech 6:9-15). Justin Martyr claimed both the Hebrew scriptures and Babylonian Joshua revealed in parable the mystery of Christ (*Dialogue With Trypho*, 65). Moreover, it was Joshua who performed certain miracles such as bringing down the wall of Jericho, and dividing of the river Jordan.

In *Melchizedek*, we learn that Joshua ben Joseph, the Jewish baby, was conceived just as other babies before, and since. Except that this particular baby was the incarnation of Michael of Nebanon (Michael-Christ story), a divine Son of Paradise. And this local universe of things and beings in this Paradise is described as an otherworldly Isle where the Absolute of the material-gravity control of the First Source and Center exists, and is motionless, and is the only stationary place in the universe, something like Aristotle's Unmoved Mover locale. Moreover, this mystery of the incarnation of Deity within the human form of Jesus, otherwise of natural origin of the world, will forever remain unsolved. Even in eternity you will never know the technique and method of the incarnation of the Creator in the form and likeness of his creatures. This is the secret of Sonarington, and such mysteries are the exclusive possession of those divine sons who have passed through the bestowal experience. According to the Michael Christ story, Sonarington is one of the seven sacred worlds of the Father. This world is the "bosom of the Son," the personal receiving world of the eternal Son. This is the Paradise headquarters of the descending and ascending Sons of God when, and after, they are fully accredited, and finally approved. Now, Osman asks "that if the historical Jesus, otherwise known as Joshua [as he so aptly describes], lived, suffered and died in the fourteenth century B.C. [*Mel.* does not provide this dating], what motives lay behind the orthodox Christian church's identification of the spiritual appearances of Christ to some of his disciples and to St. Paul-reported to have taken place during the first century A.D.-as representing the historical Jesus? Those motives were nothing less than the Church of Rome's need to situate the incarnate Jesus-the Jesus of flesh and blood-A.D. 1, and to ratify these spiritual appearances as manifestations of the historical Jesus, in order to legitimize its authority" (*Christianity, An Ancient Egyptian Religion*, 189-90). Osman gives no indication in his book that he is aware of the fantastical Michael-Christ story. A story that puts Michael, as foretold by Gabriel, as one of the seven archangels who foretold the birth of John the Baptist, even announcing the conception of the Lord to the Blessed Virgin Mary, as the reigning Christ figure in the form of Immanuel, and then Michael, on orders from Machiventa Melchizedek for some three hundred million years B.C. Recall that Jesus informed Ganid that the teachings of Melchizedek presented the clearest form of the Lord God than any other religion. It should be noted that these divine sons, including Jesus, went to great lengths to contrive their career as harbingers of truth to mankind, in such a way as to create discrepancies, and inconsistencies in their teachings to prevent others from honoring them in place of the Absolute Father. Their teachings were to Love the Father; their teachings were a helpmeet but that is all, and to forge a fruitful context, these divine Sons went to extraordinary lengths to confuse their followers. Needless to say, they all succeeded, as I stated earlier, there are, as of 2000 A.D., 2,045 conflicting stories about Jesus, and my version(s) here simply add to the confusion, indeed, complexity of this very great, but wondrous enigma.

So close to the Mithraic teaching is Christianity that I would be remiss leaving out this seeming connection. While Paul's following of Christianity encompasses the unwavering morality of Judaism and the philosophical reasoning of the Greeks, it bears an uncanny similarity to the Mithraic doctrines of atonement, salvation by the sacrifice made by a god, and redemption. Christianity being so thoroughly ensconced in the Jewish tradition, and concomitant mystery cults, it's no wonder that the Jewish Jesus cult embraced the Persian mystery cult Mithras, which was growing in popularity from the beginning of the first century until 350 years later, eventually being adopted by the Roman emperor, Constantine, when it became a dominant religion of the Roman Empire; Constantine, being the second Roman emperor after emperor Commodus to adopt (Commodus became an initiate) the Mithras teaching.

Mithras was perceived as being a god associated with light and the sanctity of oaths in India and Iran. The mysteries were celebrated by small groups of male initiates in underground temples, lined on either side by benches used for ritual meals and dominated by a representation of the god slaying the primal bull. Dying out in the fourth century C.E., being thoroughly subsumed by Christianity, it did, however, make its mark on the Christian tradition, and possibly explained how Christianity could accelerate at such a rapid rate without having a charismatic leader to drive it, assuming, of course, as some do, that Jesus was only a mythological figure. For example, in the same way Mithras became a dominant religion in the ancient world, approximately around 100 C.E., without having a leader to inspire it, so could Christianity develop into a major religion without there being a historical Jesus. The latter point, as stated, assumes one believes Jesus was only a myth, like Mithras. Without Christianity Mithras may have prevailed some say.

African Church Father (160 c.e.- 225c.e.), Tertullian, had this to say about the Mithras Mystery: "The devil, whose business is to pervert the truth, mimics the exact circumstances of the Divine Sacraments [St. Augustine of Hippo described the Sacraments as the visible forms of invisible grace]. He baptizes his believers and promises forgiveness of sins from the Sacred Fount, and thereby, initiates them into the religion of Mithras. St. Justin Martyr, an Apologist, was also accusatory toward the Mithras religion, stating they even imitated the Eucharist right down to the commemoration "This is my body...."

Going back to Jesus' travels with Ganid, this time in Corinth, Jesus and Ganid did meet an earnest follower of the Mithras, and Jesus had this to say to the follower:

> "You do well to seek for a religion of eternal salvation, but you err to go in quest of such a glorious truth among man-made mysteries and human philosophies. Know you not the mystery of human salvation dwells within your own soul? Do you not know that the God of heaven has sent his spirit to live within you, and that this spirit will lead all truth-loving and God-serving mortals out of this life and through the portals of death up to the eternal heights of light where God waits to receive his children? And never forget: You who know God are the sons of God if you truly yearn to be like him" (*Melchizedek*, 1474).

Emerging from the Gnostic tradition and retaining their affinity for the inner mysteries of Christianity acquired from the Gnostics, were St. Gregory of Nazianzum (c.e. 329/30-389-90 c.e.), St. Gregory of Nyssa (c.e.330-395) and Nyssa's brother, St. Basil the Great (c.e. 330-379c.e.), all three of whom contributed to prominent religious texts for the Eastern Orthodox Religion. All three were Cappadocian (an ancient country located in E Asia Minor: later a Roman province) Fathers of the Eastern Orthodox Christian Church. Gregory of Nyssa's exegetical works dealt extensively with the mystical sense of the scriptures.

A brief comment on the nature of myth may be helpful at this point. Joseph Campbell misappropriated some Greek myths pregnant with meaning reflective of his own psychological projection of what the myth meant in modern phraseology, instead of keeping to the actual meaning likely intended by the gods. For example, in

Ronne Gleason

Homer's *Odyssey*, Campbell says Circe sends Odysseus to the land of the dead to acquire a deeper knowledge of sexuality, when in fact, Odysseus, in obliging the realist quality of the story/myth, is going to the underworld to find out about his return home. This point is proven by the prophet (character in story line) Tiresias who never mentions anything about sexuality. Thus, by trying to invoke a modern pattern of interpretation to myth, he overlooks the fact that every myth must be taken, not simply from the context/culture in which is was spawned, but also, the time in which it was created because, like a dream (which is filled with archetypes seeded by one's immediate life's circumstances), myth must be studied from the form in which it is being expressed. That is, in Greek culture, often times the gods do not care about the affairs of men, other times they do, and while poets like Homer and Hesiod are inspired to teach man many things about life, they always seek to instruct that there are often times forces beyond one's control, and, **unlike** the myths of Mithras or Jesus, the Greek gods are more often than not, selfish and non-caring about humans, whom they consider inferior. Campbell, and other expositors of myth, attempted to create grandiose motifs coloring the motives and causations even with intimations of divinity, when in reality, Homer and Hesiod had intended no ancillary meaning at all. I suspect Nietzsche could have culled much of his nihilism/atheism from Greek stories; His volume, *The Birth of Tragedy*, suggests this. Just like real life, sometimes there is no meaning to what one does. Many myths describe the world the way it is, and not the way one would like it to be. Now, keep in mind the context, this is Greek culture which is known to be fatalistic, and so brutally down to earth, pessimism can creep into one's psyche darkening one's outlook on life. Not for Socrates though, when he knew he was about to die he uttered that God cared for him.

This does not overlook the idea that through Plato's Vision of Er, a myth described in his 10th *Book of the Republic*, we find the basic frame of the world for Greek mythology. In it we find Er, who was resurrected from the funeral pyre just before it was kindled, and who describes his travel through the other world (10.615): He and the group of souls bound for rebirth make their journey through this other world. They come through a "straight shaft of light, like a pillar, stretching from above throughout heaven and earth, and there, at the middle of the light, they saw stretching from heaven the extremities of its chains, for this light binds the heavens, holding together all the revolving firmament like the undergirths of a ship of war. And from the extremities stretched the Spindle of Necessity, by means of which all the circle revolve."

And while this myth informs of necessity/Fate as being a central law of nature, it does allow, in fact, even inspires other worldly contemplation, a key tenet of myth creation in early Christianity and Gnosticism: "for this light binds the heavens."

Now, my point in the above is to show a contrast to the Mithras and Jesus myth, wherein these two myths were designed exclusively (not always the case in Greek stories) to create a focus for contemplation of spiritual truths; to create in one a deepened feeling about a particular matter aimed toward engaging the Active Imagination, the very vehicle needed to experience a transport of consciousness away from the body, away from the earth. I am not suggesting that the study of Homer and Hesiod cannot do the same, but that is not their sole purpose, at least in the isolated example I presented. For example, the Gnostics knew that their mythical figures were the product of the imagination. In fact, the Active Imagination I discussed earlier is a common spiritual practice of the Gnostics. Myth in this regard serves to knock on the door of one's psyche breaking down its wall so the light of God can enter. Hence Imagination has given form to that which would not have form otherwise. Carl Yung developed a psychoanalytic technique based on the very same Active Imagination he learned from the Gnostics in which the patient enters into an objective relationship with the images found in their inner world.

Yung himself experienced meeting an inner teacher called Philemon, of whom he wrote: "Philemon and other figures of my fantasies brought home to me the crucial insight that there were things in the psyche *which I do not produce, and themselves, have their own life;* " adding, "Dreams are private myths. Myths are public dreams" (*Symbols of Transformation*, 5.26-29).

Another way to view the Jesus story that I will touch on only briefly, due to the magnitude of the subject, is the mystical-symbolic-occult way. In this way we interpret many portions of scripture symbolically. For example, in *Revelation* 1:11, authored by John (Justin Martyr suggests that this John is the apostle John, son of Zebedee), we find a reference to the seven churches: "Write in a book what you see and send it to the seven churches, to Ephesus, to Smyrna, to Pergamum, to Thyatira, to Sardis, to Philadelphia, and to Laodicea." Now from the perspective of western terminology these seven churches symbolize the seven ductless glands or the seven chakras (wheels of light-filled energy, and the etheric counterpart of their respective gland) in eastern terminology. For example: pineal gland (Pergamum-sahasrara chakra-imaginative-violet); pituitary gland (Smyrna-Ajna chakra-intuitive-indigo); thyroid gland (Philadelphia-vissuddha chakra-conceptual-blue); thymus gland (Thyatria-anahata chakra-acquisitive-green); adrenal gland (Ephesus-manipura chakra-intellectual-yellow); female gonads-muladhara chakra-physical sensation-red (Sardis); and the male gonads (Laodicea-muladhara chakra as in the female-physical sensation-red).

The human aura, which extends out from the physical body seventeen inches, acts as a series of spherical concentric energy centers rotating like wheels with curved spikes projecting out from the circumference, connected by subtle energies to the seven nerve centers and their ganglions, and also the seven glands of the endocrine system. Because the human body acts like a collection of raindrops, erewhile acting as spherical prisms to filter the cosmic light rays, and since pigment is reflected sunlight, primary light is thereby absorbed and re-radiated as biological radio-magnetic light. This is how our body (most specifically the endocrine system and associated mental patterns listed above) remains in intimate contact with the sun, and is also why our conscious behavior can have an actual beneficial effect on the sun as the Gurdjieff teaching espouses. In short, these chakras or glands operate as transmitting and receiving stations for various subtle energy frequencies within the body, and also from the environment, such as the magnetic fields created by all living organisms, including all magnetic fields produced by electricity, the distribution of Prana (breath) throughout the body via pneumagastric nerves and other subtle energy meridians, and finally, the translation of this breath-life force into electrochemical impulses for the body's cells.

To give you a sense of the power of magnetic fields, consider the simple microwave oven. The entire microwave oven's dynamic is based on electromagnetic waves vibrating at 2.4 billion times a second while grabbing water molecules (recall that the human body acts as a collection of raindrops) to shake them up. Water is extracted from the food, and if nothing is left in the oven for it to cook, an explosion would occur. Well, the body is mostly water. Amazingly, no heat is involved, yet look at what it does to the food! The genesis of this teaching, while emergent in esoteric/ symbolic Christianity, came from the much earlier Vedas and the Upanishads with traces evident in Tibetan Buddhism.

Each chakra or church boasts its own field of consciousness or kosa, often written as koshas. See above for associated mental field(s) of perception. These kosas are like lampstands of individual consciousness, referred to as the "seven golden lampstands" in *Revelation* 2:1., and are like sheaths of consciousness folded one within the other as you would find in the common onion skin/skin(s). As we learn from the Gurdjieff work, we tend to identify with these sheaths of perception thinking we are them, either individually or en masse (Paul admonishes "You are not your body"), thus obscuring our perception. That is, we project out our perception based on one of, or a collection of, these sheaths of awareness, thereby preventing us from experiencing the Real I, the Essence, the Soul, that would otherwise tap into the body kesdjan spiraling it/Essence outside the realm of the physical body while maintaining a state of consciousness. When John had his vision of Christ in *Revelation* 1:12, in verse 15, he says "...his voice was like the sound of many waters," he is alluding to the sound one hears upon visitation to specific planes in the invisible world. This is also my personal experience.

Fyodor Dostoevsky was forever engrossed in the *Book of Revelation*. This chapter, more than any other chapter in his bible, was heavily black-marked with numerous margin notes. He read and read hoping to comprehend its mystery. He would have benefited enormously, I suggest, from my interpretation of just this one verse. He obliged the Eastern Christian Orthodox Tradition, a tradition that emphasizes the allegorical interpretation of scripture, though not as extreme as the pure symbolic version I expressed above, he still may have been open to it. I mention this because I know you read Dostoevsky.

For an example from the Hebrew scriptures of this symbolic interpretation of certain verses, consider "...because all must go to their eternal home, and the mourners will go about the streets before the silver cord is snapped, and the golden bowl is broken, and the pitcher is broken at the fountain, and the wheel broken at the cistern, and the dust returns to earth as it was, and the breath returns to God who gave it. Vanity of vanities says the Teacher; all is vanity" (*Ecclesiastes* 12:5-8). The meaning of the silver cord is actual as I have seen my own extended cord connected to my physical body during out of body journeys, and it measures 1/32nd-1/16 of an inch. It keeps stretching and stretching no matter how far out you travel.

This cord snaps only during physical death as the verse implies. What the umbilical cord is to the physical body, the silver cord is to the spirit body. The golden bowl, the pitcher and the wheel broken at the cistern or well, symbolize the circulation of the blood stream in/through the heart, which dips up the Life or Pranic energy from the respiratory tract and then pumps it in rhythmic quantities through the heart like a wheel with buckets on it like you would see in old time wells where you dip the bucket for water.

Let's now consider a symbolic read of two *Genesis* verses: Eden, as described in *Genesis* 2:8, is the etheric or astral plane of a finer substance than the physical plane. The garden is a grosser form of that substance, yet is called Paradise. In short, it's the astral plane or more material vehicle created for mankind at this particular stage of his involution: "And the Lord God planted a garden in Eden; and there he put the man whom he had formed. Out of the ground the Lord God made to grow every *tree* that is pleasant to the sight and good for food, the *tree* of life also in the midst of the garden, and the *tree* of the knowledge of good and evil" (*Gen.* 7-9). Considering the context of this phraseology, and from a symbolic standpoint, we can assume that Garden means the Garden of the etheric realm. Now with the garden planted eastward in Eden, as scripture informs, this suggests the sensory body area because the sun rises in the east. The anterior part of the body is always the east, as we face the sun, symbolic of the rising of our sensory currents. The back of the body is the west, that is, the setting sun, or the outgoing motor currents and their major area. The top of the head is the north pole, while the feet represent the south pole. All these circulating energy currents (something like meridians in acupuncture), are to be interpreted as the sun and moon (solar in head-two head chakras, and lunar in solar plexus) each analogous to the hot and cold Polarity Principles found in Ayurvedic medicine.

Genesis 2:15 provides the key to decoding this mystery: "The Lord God took the man and put him in the garden of Eden to till it and keep it." From this we learn that God has planted soul into the human body, a body or vessel that we are to assume enormous responsibility for keeping in good condition as we are His earth-bound bodily transmitting stations for higher energies. As humans we are literally and figuratively vehicles for exchanging higher energies to lower and lower energies to higher. The latter may qualify as a presumptive addendum, but that is what allegorical and symbolic interpretation does for the one contemplating its deeper and finer mysteries. This is gnosis; this is Gnosticism, the early arm of Eastern Christian Orthodoxy.

Finally, the three trees referenced in *Genesis* 1:7-9 expounded above, symbolize the three gunas, or the three energies in their mode of motion. The tree of life is an inverted tree, with its branches growing downward and its roots toward heaven above. Symbolically, this is why man is never comfortable on earth always seeking an escape. On earth he is literally upside down. This tree is situated in the body at the central axis of the brain and spinal cord down to the second lumbar vertebra making it the cerebrospinal axis and keenly associated with the cerebrospinal fluids. The brain is the root of the tree from where the higher energies descend, hence the built in inversion stated earlier.

The tree of good food represents the fiery energies of the digestive system, which separates the gross food, and extracts the fine fiery substance out for nourishment. Interestingly, the Greeks attributed this function to Saturn who devoured his own children because life lives on life in all lower creation, just as the persistent life of our numerous individual I's, we fuel with our incessant associations/identifications with our myriad I's, preclude us from reaching our single Real I, because, instead of eating these myriad I's to lighten the mental baggage (bare our attention to strip personality of mental stuff, thus starving these I's to death) we eat gross food substances which do not require effort or sacrifice, e.g., sacrifice of some I's.

The tree of knowledge of good and evil symbolizes the procreative impulse. It includes the bodily fluids and all watery secretions in the body. Jupiter is entrusted with this function according to Greek astronomy. It is situated at the end of the spinal cord where it branches out into numerous spinal nerves called "Cauda Equina" or horse's tail. This is just below the tree of life. This is also the sensory area for the procreative impulses.

Conflating scriptural interpretation as a symbolic gesturing toward the physical body is important contextually as seen in these two examples, because, unlike the Greek context found in my first scenario, we can surmise the scribes and Paul or Jesus, intended a deeper, non-literal rendering of their words. We know Paul admonishes us to "Know that your body is a temple of the Holy Spirit" (1 *Cor.* 6:19); or "God's temple is sacred, and you are that temple (1 *Cor.* 3:17). The above interpretations, however limited their scope due to the nature of this letter, captures this theme of the body, and its importance in Christian theology.

I will now cover the physiology of the Cross by Plato in lieu of your sardonic reference to its significance or lack of. In St. Justin Martyr's *First Apology* he titles Chapter L X-*Plato's Doctrine of the Cross*, wherein Plato is seen describing his affinity for the Cross and its power. It reads:

> And the physiological discussion concerning the Son of God in the Timaeus of Plato, where he [Plato] says, "He placed him crosswise in the universe;" this he borrowed in like manner from Moses; for in the writings of Moses it is related how at that time, when the Israelites went out of Egypt and were in the wilderness, they fell in with poisonous beasts, both vipers and asps, and every kind of serpent which slew the people; and that Moses, by inspiration and influence of God, **took brass, and made it into a figure of the cross**, and set it in the holy tabernacle, and said to the people, "If ye look to

this figure, and believe, ye shall be saved thereby." And when this was done, it was recorded that the serpents died, and it is handed down that the people thus escaped death. Which things Plato was reading, and not accurately understanding, and not apprehending that it was the figure of the cross, but taking it to be a placing crosswise, he [Plato] said that the power next to the first God was placed crosswise in the universe. And as to his speaking of a third, he did this because he read, as we said above, that which was spoken by Moses, "that the Spirit of God moved over the waters." For he gives the second place to the Logos which is with God, who he said was placed crosswise in the universe; and the third place to the Spirit who was said to be borne upon the water saying, "and the third around the third" (*Ante-Nicene* Fathers, vol. 1, pg. 182.). Note: The Ante-Nicene period covers the first 325 yrs. c.e., the period you expressed an interest in Jerry.

In the same way the pyramids espouse an extraordinary power through their unique mathematical configuration, i.e. geometry, so is Plato asking that we perceive the cross in like manner: "crosswise in the universe." His theory of the Platonic Solids is based on the power of geometric configuration.

The cross never existed historically; and it was Protonica, the wife of Emperor Claudius (d.A.D.54), who may have been the first person to have discovered it during the reign of her uncle Tiberius who ruled from A.D. 14-37, when she is said to have forced the Jews to hand over the hill of Golgotha, the very hill where Jesus was crucified, at which time she uncovered the cross. Protonica convinced her daughter to make this Cross searching journey to Jerusalem from Rome with her. Once Protonica found the cross, a short time afterwards her daughter suddenly died, but was mysteriously restored to life once her corpse was placed on this Cross.

Another account has Helena, the mother of Emperor

Constantine, in A.D. 325, as the finder of the 'true cross.' And while widely accepted as the discoverer of the 'true cross,' historians assert it was a replica of the Petronica cross. This could be why renowned literalist historian, Eusebius (c.260-c.340-Bp. of Caesarea by 315), published Petronica's discovery in the Doctrina Addai; Addai being one of the 72 disciples of Jesus. However, to complicate the certainty of the actual discoverer of the 'true cross,' Helena's discovery, likewise being on the hill of Golgotha, also experienced a miracle when, upon laying a crippled person on the 'cross,' recovered miraculously (*Christianity, An Ancient Egyptian Religion*, Ahmed Osman, pgs. 231-33).

Early Christian symbols of the cross represented the Egyptian ankh, the symbol of eternal spiritual life. The standard ankh cross is a circle above a T cross. This is probably because the circle symbolizes the eternity of time or eternal recurrence, a very common theme in the Gurdjieff work and Nietzschean ideology. Also, the circle is a symbol of the archetypical cosmos or pleroma in Christian terminology, as contrasted by the kenoma, or physical cosmos of duality. In the circle is seen the two as One, whereas the stick descending down from where the circle meets the top of the cross, symbolizes the One as two. Osman says it was Rome who replaced the ankh with the Latin-Roman cross, a symbol of punishment, in the fifth century.

For me the cross has a powerful meaning. During an exorcism I was asked to perform for a friend of my brother's thirty years ago, whom was heavily possessed by negative spirits, I, upon making the symbol of the cross, witnessed the spirit being expelled from the individual almost instantaneously, much to the relief of the person, and myself. It seemed that the cross construct trumped my other efforts.

In consideration of this extensive briefing on the historicity of Christianity and various ways of viewing scripture, I will now provide an illuminating, very poignant quote from Nietzsche's work,

Ronne Gleason

On the Uses and Disadvantages of History for Life:

Modern theology in particular seems to have devoted itself to the study of history out of pure naivete, and even now it tries to ignore that, by so doing it serves, no doubt quite unwillingly, Voltaire's *Ecrasez*.... What can be learned from Christianity is that it has become apathetic and unnatural through historicizing treatment, and in the end totally historical-that is, a just treatment has reduced it to pure knowledge about Christianity, thereby destroying it. This same process can be observed in connection with any living thing...it becomes painfully sick the moment we begin to dissect it historically.... Imagine transporting a few of these modern biographers to the birthplace of Christianity or the Lutheran Reformation; their cold, pragmatic curiosity would be just enough to render every spiritual *actio in disans* quite impossible-just as the most pitiful animal can, by eating the acorn, prevent the mightiest oak from sprouting. Every living thing needs a surrounding atmosphere, **a shrouding aura of mystery**. [My emphasis]. If this shroud is removed, if a religion, an art, a genius is condemned to move like a star without an atmosphere, no wonder they soon harden, dry up, and cease to bear. So it is with all great things "which never without some illusion prosper," as Hans Sachs puts it in *Die Meisterersinger*, (Nietzsche, 7).

Ironically, Nietzsche was educated as a philologist and historian, yet it was historical analysis and arguments that contributed mostly to his break with Christianity. So for Nietzsche historical investigation will **always** destroy faith and religion, in addition to art and poetry. More on Nietzsche later.

The debate between science and religion, between atheism and theism, between a purposive universe and nihilism, has been going on since the beginning of time. To cast an illuminating light on this controversy I will provide positions taken by David Hume (1711-1776), a very worthy skeptic, Mark Twain (1835-1910), and Friedrich Nietzsche (1844-1900). I'll begin with Hume, and the fact that he was a skeptic will prove instructive to the fact that in his brief autobiography, *In My Own Life*, in which he asserts that his personal narrative shall contain a little more than a history of his writings, leaves out any mention of his *Dialogues* (a critique of religion), a manuscript that he had worked on from as early as 1751, revising several details of it by 1761, and again in 1776, when he knew he was approaching death. Copying Plato's idea that utilizing dialogue was a good approach to communicate ideas, he engages the character of Philo, pitted against Cleanthes, to debate theism versus atheism. Some scholars conclude that Hume is most likely Philo in this dialogue. I opine it is Cleanthes, but as I will show, both characters are not that far apart in their opinions: In a letter Hume wrote to Gilbert Eliot in 1751 regarding the *Dialogues*, he stated that he could have kept his temper well being either Philo or Cleanthes; adding both characters are him. A portion of the dialogue is as follows:

> Philo speaks thus: I ask the theist, if he does not allow, that there is a great and immeasurable, because incomprehensible, difference between the human and divine mind: The more pious he is, the more readily will he assent to the affirmative, and the more will he be disposed to magnify the difference: he will even assert, that the difference is of a nature which cannot be too much magnified. I next turn to the atheist, who, I assert, is only nominally so, and can never be in earnest; and I ask him, whether, from the coherence and apparent sympathy in all the parts of this world, there be not a certain degree of analogy among all the operations of nature, in every situation, and in every age; whether the rot-

ting of a turnip, the generation of an animal, and the structure of human thought be not energies that bear some remote analogy to each other: It is impossible he can deny it: He will readily acknowledge it. Having obtained this concession, I will push him still farther in his retreat; and I ask him, if it be not probable that the principle which first arranged, and still maintains, order in this universe, bears not also some inconceivable analogy to the other operations of nature, and among the rest to economy of human mind and thought. However reluctant, he must give his consent. Where then cry I to both these antagonists, is the subject of your dispute? The theist allows that the original intelligence is very different from human reason: The atheist allows that the original principle of order bears some remote analogy to it. Will you quarrel gentleman, about the degrees, and enter into a controversy, which admits not of any precise meaning, nor consequently of any determination? If you should be so obstinate, I should not be surprised to find you insensibly change sides; while the theist, on the one hand, exaggerates the dissimilarity between the supreme Being, and frail, imperfect, variable, fleeting, and mortal creatures; and the atheist, on the other hand, magnifies the analogy among all operations of nature, in every period, every situation, and every position. Consider then, where the real point of controversy lies, and if you cannot set aside your disputes, endeavor at least, to cure yourselves of your animosity.

And here I must also acknowledge Cleanthes, ...as the supreme Being is allowed to be absolutely and entirely perfect, whatever differs most from him departs the farthest from the supreme standard of rectitude and perfection.

Philo, after stating that these were his unfeigned sentiments on this subject, added, "But in proportion to my veneration for true religion, is my abhorrence of vulgar superstition; and I indulge a peculiar pleasure, I confess, in pushing such principles, sometimes into absurdity, sometimes into impiety." Cleanthes replies thus: "Religion, however corrupted, is still better than no religion at all. The doctrine of a future state is so strong and necessary a security to morals, that we aught never abandon or neglect it. For if finite and temporary rewards and punishments have such great an effect, as we daily find: how much greater must be expected from such as are infinite and eternal." Philo replies by emphasizing that in the name of vulgar superstition (false religion), wars and violence erupt all over, and that a natural honesty and benevolence has more effect on a person's conduct than views suggested by theological theories and systems. To this thought he adds: "True religion, I allow, has no such pernicious consequences; but we must treat of religion, as it has commonly been found in the world...." Cleanthes replies: "The proper office of religion is to regulate the hearts of men, humanize their conduct, infuse the spirit of temperance, order and obedience; and as its operation is silent, and only enforces the motives of morality and justice, it is in danger of being overlooked, and confounded with these other motives. When it distinguishes itself, and acts as a separate principle over men, it has departed from its proper sphere [as in true religion absent hypocrisy], and has become only a cover to faction and ambition" (120-21). Later in the dialogue Philo confesses that the existence of a deity is "plainly ascertained by reason" (133).

Interestingly, in Hume's earlier work, *Natural History of Religion*, an exposition of the origin of human nature, its nature and causes, he states in the *Introduction* the following, "The whole frame of nature bespeaks an intelligent author; and no rational enquirer, after serious reflection, can suspend his belief a moment with regard to the primary virtues of genuine Theism and Religion." By this statement we can either assume he is suggesting, as some scholars assert, that he opines religion is very unattractive, its realness notwithstanding, or to embrace a healthy philosophical skepticism serves the unique purpose of bringing one to true religion, a religion that can see the falsity, in Twain-like fashion, of pseudo religion, wherein, its followers are oblivious to their hypocrisy. This is the negative side of the quote; the positive side would say Hume, in his later years as he nears death, is surrendering to the idea that there is a God, and moreover, his affirmation is to be taken literally.

Being a renowned skeptic, Hume has to be resistant to admitting that he is an atheist, not only because of its obvious societal inconvenience for him in philosophical circles, but also, because to arrive at any conclusion as certain as atheism, would require a suspension of his skeptical reasoning used in his philosophical writings; he is skeptical of science for this same reason; but he does go on to say in the *Dialogues* that of one thing he is certain is that there is a God; of course, he had already said as much through Philo.

It appears Mark Twain, shortly before his own death, in adding two chapters to his infamous, iconoclastic tale, *Captain Stormfield's Visit to Heaven*, titled *Extract from Captain Stormfield's Visit to Heaven*, modified some of the effects of the blasphemous intimations evident in his original tale, suggesting his reticence to offend believers and a God he believed in, and maybe even feared: "We know that the real God, the Supreme God, the actual Maker of the universe, made everything that is in it... He made it an unchanging law that the creature should suffer wanton and unnecessary pains and miseries everyday of his life-that by that law these pains and miseries could not be avoided by any diplomacy exercisable by the creature...And that by another law every transgression of a law of Nature, either ignorantly or wittingly committed, should in every instance be visited by a punishment ten-thousand-fold out of proportion to the transgression" (*The Bible According to Mark Twain, from Concerning the Character of the Real God*, June 25, 1906, p.325). In this quote Twain assumes he can judge/assess the degree of one's transgressions not realizing that maligned thoughts alone can justify punishment, and no man can assess the extent of another's private thoughts, positive or negative. I opine, one can suffer these punishments years, or even lifetimes after the transgression. And this is done to prevent one from figuring out the method in which God works to punish his creatures; this way He seeks to convey the message that sometimes you may think you have gotten away with the transgression, when in fact, God, as He says, knows all things and every deed, or mis-deed, will deal with the matter in His own way, His own time. In this manner those who perform the transgressions who think they are getting away with something, and even after years of escaping punishment, suddenly come to the realization that even if they can get away with the transgression, right their ways anyway, in the name of simply doing the right thing, or doing the right thing for God's sake. So without God having to shake his fist at the transgressor, he/she made the correction on their own; this is the way God prefers i.e., via one's own free will. To confuse this scenario, punishment can occur instantly.

Now, after withholding the revisions for publication for some thirty years, for aforementioned reasons, he presented part of it to *Harper's Magazine's* editor, George Harvey who proclaimed that the Extract was "too damn godly." *Harper's Magazine* was/is a secular magazine. Happily for Twain, Harvey changed his mind one year later, and published the two *Extract* chapters in December's 1907 and January 1908 issues. In October 1909 *Harper's* published E*xtract from Captain Stormfield's Visit to Heaven* as a **Christmas Gift Book** stretching the approximately 15,000 words of text out over 121 pages. As we found in Hume's *Dialogues*, we also find in Twain's *Extract*, it becoming the very last publication in his lifetime. Could it be, as Paul the apostle says, that God is written in the hearts of all people, and while we may attempt to outrun this inheritance, we will fail if we are fortunate. I surmise both Hume and Twain were fortunate.

Ronne Gleason

In the *Extract* we find in chapter four how Heaven proves to be a place in which humans learn how significant their world is in the larger scheme of things. In chapter six we learn that prayers are always answered, and quickly in Heaven time: One thousand years of earth is equivalent to only a day in Heaven. Being very well versed in the Bible, Twain culled this idea from *Psalms* 90:4: "For a thousand years in your sight are like yesterday when it is past." Consequently, what seems a slow response to us (one minute in Heaven is equivalent to one year on earth), is actually quick in Heaven time.

Another interesting passage from the *Extract* that was preserved in the manuscript but deleted from the typescript or proof submitted, is the original Mrs. Rushmore and Daughter episode. The following is the complete deletion:

> "How you talk! Would heaven be heaven if you couldn't slander folks? Come to think, I don't believe it would-for some people-but I hadn't thought of it before."
>
> "For some people?—There you hit it. The trouble on earth is, that they leave out the *some-people* class-they try to fix up a heaven for only one kind of people. It won't work. There are all kinds here-and God cares for all kinds. He makes all happy; if he can't do it in one way, he does it in another. He doesn't leave anybody out in the cold" (*The Bible According to Mark Twain*, 302. H. Baetzhold and J. McCullough, E05.).

It is believed that Twain left out this episode because he thought it was too sentimental or because he did not want to create problems by using the name Mrs. Rushmore. Shortly before the story went to press, Twain was treated for bronchitis by a doctor named Dr. Edward C. Rushmore, who opined Twain needed an operation, but he was too old. While pure coincidence, Twain may have thought the doctor would think he was inappropriately using his name, especially considering that the last three lines allude to being tended to.

Because you and I have touched on *Captain Stormfield's Visit to Heaven* tale (You affirming you knew it was a satire), and because Twain liked to poke fun at religion, I thought you would find the intimations of the *Extract* interesting, if not revealing of Twain's late in life attitudes toward religion. Twain suffered profound ambivalence for thirty years over the original *Captain Stormfield* tale, and its severely blasphemous nature; it appears that by adding the two chapters, now known as the *Extract from Captain Stormfield's Visit to Heaven*, he assuaged a troubled conscience, a conscience fed by years of studying the Bible, a book that influenced him more than any other book according to critics. He sensed its many fallacies, but he could not have devoted so much study time to a work, and then filter its themes throughout the entirety of his writings, unless the book had a positive impact. His iconoclastic angst over the Bible could have merely been his wish that it was more consistent, less riddled in incomprehensible perplexities. Doubtful he would have ever admitted this; after all, he felt he had much of it figured out, at least intellectually.

Recall earlier in this letter I mentioned that Jesus intentionally sought to weave his themes around confusing anomalies to keep the majority from grasping the deeper meaning(s). And, by doing this, he kept followers from worshiping him direct(ly); he wanted people to worship his Father in heaven, not him. Moreover, can it not be said that to insure one's immortality (a central intent of any pivotal religious figure), one must need create riddles impossible to decipher, yet enigmatic enough to keep people trying forever with little result? Consider these brilliant lines of James Joyce referencing his immortal novel, *Ulysses*: "I've put in so many enigmas and puzzles that it will keep professors busy for centuries arguing over what I meant, and that's the only way of insuring one's immortality."

There is a myth in Judaism propounded by Eleazar that revolves around two men arguing about the powers of God. One man says to the other if you are so divine then create a tree right from this ground we are standing on. The man performs this miracle a couple of times, but never to the satisfaction of the doubter due to the fact that the guardian, all seeing spirit, Eleazar is watching this conversation from the other world, and seeks to intentionally prevent the miraculous creation of the one man from having any satisfactory influence on the doubter. The one man beseeches Eleazar to confirm the reality of his miraculous creation but he refuses to do so. Eleazar eventually tells both men that God is not about creating miracles, rather, it's about remembering Him; it's about talking about Him; it's about arguing about Him. This way He knows He will never be forgotten. I have paraphrased the gist of this from memory. My Harvard professor in Judaism handed out to the class the original rare script of this myth that spawned the core element in Judaism. This moment in class, and follow up discussion, served as an epiphany for me about Judaism and why argument about God was/is so integral to their religion, even all their warring antagonisms could serve this purpose, even if its killing others in holy wars, at least God is being remembered. So I pondered/ponder!

One more word on Twain's anger over God's ways. In John Milton's poem, *Paradise Lost*, he seeks to justify the ways of God to men; and like Leibniz, in my opinion, purports a psychologically gripping theodicy that is inspiring, if not enlightening. These potent lines from the poem give the flavor of its content and shadow Twain's derision:

> What in me is dark,
> Illumine, what is low, raise and support;
> That to the height of this great argument
> I may assert eternal providence,
> And justify the ways of God to men (65:10).

Letters to a Skeptic

Now we come to Nietzsche. His corpus of contrarieties is so vast he has learned the art of saying many things by saying what he didn't say. Instead of expanding old familiar ideas, he expounded from behind them. That is, he attempted to understand the ancient text (and its familiar message) better than the author who drafted it. In doing this he was able to shift perspectives and transport the meaning of the text into the foreign ground; and thus, by engaging this practice he could render the text unfamiliar to himself, and hopefully, derive a brand new perspective, something like might happen when you leave your home or friend that you have become accustomed to (overly familiar with) for a year or more, and then, upon returning, you discover that you can view the home or friend fresh, and maybe even acquire a brand new insight that was not possible before, and this time, without any subjective sensations. My opening line 'saying many things by saying what he didn't say,' is more aptly stated thus: whenever a person tells us something about him/herself, what is said revelation supposed to conceal? What prejudice is it suppose to arouse, whether it be of an individual or an IDEA? Einstein once said that to be able to view things in "opposites" is a sign of genius. Interestingly, many of Nietzsche's ideas are Sufi-like, and the art of looking behind a matter is needed to better understand Sufi stories, a prominent teaching device they incorporate for enhancing self understanding. Also because Nietzsche had a profound grasp of depth psychology, something he probably culled from studying Sophocles' plays, the acclaimed first depth psychologist, I suggest much of Nietzsche's religious writings should be viewed from the perspective of his attempt to de-familiarize, de-program, de-condition or de-automate himself to all his religious upbringing (Luther) and conditioning. Nietzsche scholar, Lou Salome, said of Nietzsche that he should be read as a religious writer. In *On the Genealogy of Morals* we learn of Nietzsche's admission that he lived and wrote by the light of a flame ignited by the ancient fire of the Christian faith, which faith was also Plato's, that God is truth, and that truth is divine (152).

Santaniello embellishes this Nietzschean position, adding "Our gods may now be dead-as dead as he [Nietzsche] pronounced at least one of them to be, as dead as the quite human priests of our racial history, as dead as Siddhartha, Jesus, Luther-but the shade-like shadows of all these figures, Nietzsche insisted, linger in the form of their effects on our evolution from homo natura into homo religiosi" (*Nietzsche and the Gods*, (159).

As Paul the Apostle said, God is written in our hearts, so is Nietzsche saying as much when he proclaims, in *Gay Science*, that while the biological evolutionary aspect of homines religiosi was not found in "the wild beast species," they lacking in consciousness (354), and subject to chance selective forces that played with their future in a game in which no hand, not even "a finger of God took part" (*Beyond Good and Evil*, 203), it evolved into what Nietzsche called a new type of human being with social dispositions that fostered consciousness, whereupon an active intellectual life arose, and the most telling of judgments for Nietzsche, notes Santaniello, "are those of a religious nature: we become disciplined agents who become so conscientious in meeting the unconditional duties of piety that we can countermand our deepest impulses, as shown by our bouts of social withdrawal, fasting, and sexual abstinence, all performed in the name of God. If it were not for our religions, we would still be Kantian animals ruled by affect and desire, incapable of giving our word to the wisp of air we call a promise" (*BGE*, Nietzsche, 160).

For Nietzsche, as Santaniello points out, we are all Buddhists, Christians, Jews, Sikhs, Muslims or Hindus, and the fact that the gods that we knew them as are dead ("God is dead," proclaimed Nietzsche) is irrelevant, but what is relevant is that incorrect images of these religions fostered by uninformed, or simply patronizing priests to enlarge their flocks, and religious teachers in general, have bred us into a religious animal, a savage driven by our passions, pinned in by guilt harboring a hatred of all that is earthly. In concert with Judaism, knowingly or unknowingly, Nietzsche is advocating a life affirming perspective, not the life negating perspective promulgated by the non-Jewish religious hierarchy, his contradictory verbiage notwithstanding. For Nietzsche, this perspective is foreign to his upbringing (Luther), and therefore, merits investigation because one thing he is certain of is that not only is his own German culture sick, so are most others. He blames distorted views of religion for this, not religion as it was practiced in ancient times. In a note to *Schopenhauer as Educator*, Nietzsche praises Christianity and its world-denying attitude, and as Santaneillo points out, this positive world denying attitude of Nietzsche's, has regrettably become almost completely worldly, in other words, contrary to the anti-world asceticism of the early Fathers, a teaching Nietzsche advocated; today, if you abstain from soda pop that is now considered world-denying. The following words of Nietzsche in his journal notes published posthumously are poignant:

> Thus is Christianity, one of the most wonderful individual revelations and forms of expression of that inexhaustible expressive world-denying culture, [Plato] gradually, in a hundred different ways, used to turn the mills of the worldly powers and therefore became hypocritical and false into its very roots (*Samtliche Werke: Kritische Studienausgabe*, vol. 7,35[12]).

Here we notice Nietzsche praising the world-denying attitude of Christianity in one breath, and then contradicting himself when he blames Plato for leading us away from life affirming principles by teaching his other-worldly (as in world-denying) doctrine, thus creating, according to Nietzsche, one of the two household gods that have gone astray, the first one being the god of Christianity or Plato god called Knowledge-Truth, a truth that demands asceticism

Ronne Gleason

(*On the Genealogy of Morals*, 111:25); the second god being Faith, a god that was enhanced by Luther, or the Reformation that emphasized faith or belief (just utter your belief and you're saved kind of thing), not works, thus eschewing the teachings of early Christianity (asceticism), a period Nietzsche embraced with strong religious fervor. In a letter that criticizes an anti-Christian essay written by religion critic, David Strauss, titled *David Strauss, the Confessor and the Writer*, we see Nietzsche in an unusual light in his attack on Strauss for maligning Christianity:

> He has forgotten the best part of Christianity, the great eremites [desert hermits very common in early Christianity] and holy men, in short, the genius [these were the Holy Fathers of early Christian Orthodoxy], and he judges like a country parson would judge art or like Kant about music (who valued it as military music).
> Strauss had turned to Christianity to destroy, by means of exposing myths. But the nature of religion consists precisely in the possession of the power and freedom to create myths. His triumph is to show contradictions with reason and the present science. He has no inkling of the profound antinomy of idealism and of the highly relative sense of all science and reason. Or: precisely reason should tell him how little reason can say about the real nature of things (*Samtliche Werke. Kritische Studienausgabe*, vol. 7,27[1]).

In these same notes Nietzsche says "Early Christianity was a much higher form than today's Christianity, which has become comfortable" (vol. 7. 30[34]). Adding that Christianity has degenerated in its failure to give existence a metaphysical meaning (vol. 7, 32[72+77 and 34[34]). Santaneillo observes that Nietzsche's penchant for the metaphysical was probably influenced by Schopenhauer's metaphysical beliefs.

While Nietzsche emphasized that there is nothing wrong with the metaphysical, that is, the religious orientations of life in *Birth of Tragedy*, adding that in fact, these methods are the only way one can make sense of existence (as pointed out by Santaniello), it is through a this-worldly grounding that one can arrive at Truth/Knowledge, not the other way around. In other words, a Truth or Knowledge that methodically probes propositions associated with the origin, nature and method of the limits of human knowing. (I ask, do not Plato's *Dialogues* exert this type of investigation)? Keep in mind that Nietzsche's method embraces the notion of deciphering an ancient text to experience the Truth it espouses by looking at what the author does not say. In the literary art of close reading, a method I was taught in one of my Harvard Philosophy and Literature classes, every paragraph a writer composes (especially applicable to ancient poetry I opine) contains hidden messages that not even the author is aware of, but they exist nonetheless, and as a result, reveal especial insights. This is what Nietzsche is saying he did in his study of ancient texts: he read behind the texts.

The contrapuntal aspects of Nietzsche is crucial to understanding him and his contradictions, contradictions that may not really be ones, they being merely counter-points with no prejudice, e.g., he has been seen as the anti-Christ figure, when in fact he longs for the re-emergence of the ancient Christian teachings proffered by the Fathers of the early church in order to set culture back on the correct path. Nietzsche rejected Luther because he thought he rejected asceticism as a way to being saved; I suggest he was not aware of *Luther's Basic Theological Writings*, wherein he states, in regard to the *second kind of righteousness*, the following: "This is that manner of life spent profitably in good works, in the first place, in slaying the flesh and crucifying the desires with respect to the self," of which we read in *Gal.* 5:24: "And those who belong to Christ Jesus have crucified the flesh with its passions and desires" (157). More on Luther later. Continuing with Nietzsche who incorrectly aligns

Plato with pure metaphysical teachings, when in fact, Plato emphasized Reason to the highest degree as we find stated in the *Introduction to his Collected Dialogues, Including the Letters*:

> But Plato saw the world to be intelligible [apprehensible by the mind], that is, he held that system pervades all things. In order to indicate the nature of that reality he resorted to story, metaphor, and playfulness which have given comfort from time to time to esoteric writers. But the difference between Plato and the mysticism that has attached itself to his philosophy is essential. Plato's aim is to take the reader by steps, with as severe a logic as the conversational method permits, to an insight into the ultimate necessity of Reason (XV).

Moreover, when Nietzsche affirms his faith in the other world, his metaphysical perspective is unveiled: "The truthful man, in an audacious and ultimate sense presupposed by the faith in science, thereby affirms another world than that of life, nature, and history; and insofar as he affirms 'this other world,' does this not mean that he has to deny its antithesis, this world, our world...? It is still a metaphysical faith that underlies our faith in science-and we men of knowledge of today, we godless men and metaphysicians, we, too, still derive our flame from the fire ignited by a faith millennia old, the Christian faith, which was Plato's, that God is truth, that truth is divine" *On The Genealogy of Morals*, 152). It appears Nietzsche, based on the above two quotations, was not aware of some key elements in his accusations against Plato and Luther. To say that Plato's god misled the people into embracing the metaphysical realms to the exclusion of a Reasoned search for Truth is completely anathema to his intention as the quote from his *Dialogues' Introduction* qualifies. In fact, in deference to Nietzsche's contrapuntal methodology, in noting his **rejection** of reason relative to the highest truth, consider his words in *On the Genealogy of Morals*:

"To renounce belief in one's ego, to deny one's own "reality"-what a triumph! not merely over the senses, over appearance, but a much higher kind of triumph, a violation and cruelty against reason-a voluptuous pleasure that reaches its height when the ascetic self-contempt and self-mockery of reason declares: there is a realm of truth and being, **but reason is excluded from it**" (118). The praise of ascetic labors and clear rejection of reason to embrace Truth/Knowledge echo qualities found in Orthodoxy.

Furthermore, for Nietzsche to say that Luther misled his followers by leading them to think that ascetic practices were not necessary for obtaining salvation is also contrary to Luther's teachings indicated by his assertion that one must "slay the flesh and crucify the desires," the very thing Nietzsche teaches in *Daybreak* in order to overcome self when he proclaims "one can dispose of one's drives like a gardener and, though few know it can also [contrariwise], cultivate the shoots of anger, pity, curiosity, vanity as productively as, and profitably as a beautiful fruit tree on a trellis; one can do it with the good or bad taste of a gardener....All this we are at liberty to do; but how many know we are at liberty to do it?" (*Daybreak*, 560).

Nietzsche's crucial ideal on how to become the Ubermensch (Superman), and thereby escape the effects of the cultural atrocities heaped on him/her from childhood, and thus home in on Truth-Knowledge, can be accomplished by, as implied in his above words, by pruning the drives as a gardener weeds his garden:

> First, one can avoid opportunities for gratification of the drive, and through long and ever longer periods of non-gratification, weaken it and make it wither away. Secondly, one can impose upon oneself strict regularity in its gratification: by thus imposing a rule upon the drive itself and enclosing its ebb and flow within firm time-boundaries, one has then gained intervals during which one is no longer troubled by it-

and from there one can perhaps go over to the first method. Thirdly, one can deliberately give oneself over to the wild and unrestrained gratification drive in order to generate disgust with it, and with disgust to acquire a power over the drive: always supposing one does not do what the rider did who rode his horse to death and broke his own neck in the process-which unfortunately, is the rule when this method is attempted. Fourthly, there is the intellectual method of associating its gratification in general so firmly with some very painful thought that, after a little practice, the thought of its gratification is itself at once felt as very painful.... Finally, he who can endure it and finds it reasonable to weaken and depress his entire body and physical organization will naturally thereby also attain the goal of weakening an individual drive: as he does, for example, who, like the ascetic, starves his sensuality and thereby also starves and ruins his vigor and not seldom his reason as well (109).

A clear Gurdjieffian and Orthodox idea found in *Twilight of the Idols* is when Nietzsche states "the first preliminary schooling in spirituality" for the spiritual aspirant is "not to react immediately to a stimulus, but to have the restraining, stock taking instincts in one's control" (6,8). Adding that the first step in self discipline is to "become master over one's wrath, one's choler and revengefulness, and one's lusts, as any attempt to become master in anything else, is as stupid as the farmer who stakes out his field beside a torrential stream without protecting himself against it" (*The Wanderer and His Shadow*, 65). To live voluntarily, that is, independent of reactive impulse, was Truth bound for Nietzsche.

After considering the first household god (Truth-Knowledge wrapped around ascetic labors) that has to be put on trial and embraced intensely for a person to become a truly developed homines religiosi, I will now discuss in brief the second household god that must endure the same trial, that god is Faith. Recall Nietzsche saying that Luther said that all a person needed was faith to be saved; and while this attitude is commonly believed by the masses, it is not totally accurate; the genesis of this inaccuracy could be Luther's emphasis on faith as taught by Paul in *Romans* as being his favored chapter in the Bible versus *James* which teaches works alongside faith ("Faith without works is dead") as being crucial to one's salvation; Luther stated *James* was a chapter of straws because it emphasized works. Where Nietzsche went wrong in interpreting Luther's emphasis is that he never decoded Luther's real message. Luther said he placed extreme emphasis on faith, as opposed to faith and works, because this way he was sure to give the message that just because one does works he is not justified by God, therefore, not saved. He knew he was taking a chance in proffering this emphasis, it being so critical to salvation he believed, that he in no way meant that works were not necessary, e.g. consider his following words:

> Although, as I have said, a man is abundantly and sufficiently justified by faith inwardly, in his spirit, and so has all that he needs, except insofar as this faith and these riches must grow from day to day even for the future life; yet he remains a mortal on this earth. In this life he must control his own and have dealings with men. **Here the work begins** [my emphasis]; here a man cannot enjoy leisure; here he must indeed take care to discipline his body by fasting(s), watching(s), labors, and other reasonable discipline and to subject it to the Spirit so that it will obey and conform to the inner man and faith and not revolt against faith and hinder the inner man, as it is the nature of the body to do if it is not held in check.... While doing this, behold, he meets a contrary will in his own flesh which strives to serve the world and seeks it own advantage. This the spirit of faith cannot tolerate, but with joyful zeal it

attempts to put the body under control and hold it in check, as Paul says in *Romans* 7: 22-23: "For I delight in the law of God, in my inmost self, but I see in my members another law at war with the law of the mind and making me captive to the law of sin", and in another place, "But I pommel my body and subdue it, lest after preaching to others I myself should be disqualified" (I *Cor.* 9:27), and in *Galatians* (5:24): "And those who belong to Christ Jesus have crucified the flesh with its passions and desires."

Nevertheless, the works themselves do not justify him before God, but he does the works out of obedience to God and considers nothing except the approval of God, whom he must scrupulously obey in all things (*Martin Luther, Selections from his Writings*, 67,68).

In these words of Luther we can see he obliges a kind of simultaneous engagement of faith and works; well, curiously, when Nietzsche was asked what did he favor faith or Knowledge-Truth which I align with Works (works being not only a this-worldly involvement, a key criteria for Nietzsche, but also a result of embracing Truth or Knowledge), he said both at the same time: "It is to take both at once" (*Nietzsche and the Gods*, Santiello, 164). Nietzsche says man with Knowledge will practice ascetic works, even seek to be an Ubermensch or Superman; his ascetic method is shown above.

How Knowledge-Truth and works parallel each other we must consider that for Nietzsche, Truth is centered around the reality that our world is an ocean of pain, not unlike the Buddhist indictment that life is Suffering. Nietzsche was drawn to Buddhism, but his slight misunderstanding of Buddhist asceticism lead him to conclude that all Buddhists must practice ascetic labors. He was not aware that the Brahmins, unlike the monastics (monks), were not suited for such labors evolutionarily or otherwise. I mention this misappropriation of ideals because it is this same attitude that led him to conclude that all Christians should practice ascetic labors, after all, just as the Buddha taught that ascetic labors were needed to rise above the suffering of life, so did Jesus teach the same. Nietzsche thought that both Buddhism and Christianity were nihilistic [Nietzsche felt nihilism was unlivable], but Buddhism more realistic (*The Antichrist*, 20,42).

As Gurdjieff and the Holy Fathers proclaim, intentional suffering (voluntary ascetic labors), while difficult in the beginning, can only lead to no suffering later, as in the freedom from pain (recall that Truth-Knowledge for Nietzsche includes knowing life is an ocean of pain) was seeded by choosing one's path of suffering, thus avoiding the ever common un-intentional suffering that equals pain for most. I sense Nietzsche knew the especial twist in this dichotomy from his words in *Daybreak*: "Indeed, happiness, conceived of as the liveliest feeling of power, has perhaps been nowhere greater on earth than in the souls of superstitious ascetics" (113). So mighty is this supervening power, alludes Nietzsche in *On the Genealogy of Morals*, said Indian ascetic can accumulate sufficient energies to enable him to think he could create a new universe, a heaven within his own hell (115); or a priest, in his unyielding effort to bridge the gap between himself and God, obliges sheer Mephistophelian zeal through "the spirit that negates... and yet creates the good" (*Faust*, Goethe, Ins. 1335); "and moreover, this priest, in his incarnate desire to be in a different place, and indeed this desire at its greatest extreme, its distinctive fervor and passion; but precisely this *power* of his desire is the chain that holds him captive so that **he becomes a tool for creation** of more favorable conditions for being here, and being man-it is precisely this power that enables him to persuade existence, the whole herd of the ill-constituted, disgruntled, underprivileged, unfortunate, and all who suffer themselves, by instinctively going before them as their **shepherd**. You will see my point: this ascetic priest, this apparent enemy of life, this *demer*-precisely he is among the greatest *conserving* and yes-creating forces of life... The No he says to life brings to light, as if by magic, an abundance of tender Yeses; even when he *wounds* himself, this master of destruction, of self-destruction-the very wound itself afterward compels him to *live*" (GM, 120-21-dated 1887; his last works being in 1888). In these inspiring lines we find the essence of Eastern Christian Orthodoxy decoded by the Holy Fathers of the ancient church whom Nietzsche revered; and he, like Hegel, blamed Judaism and its heavy dose of legal mores, for straying from this very Orthodoxy and subsequent alienation from God, from nature, and from the world, i.e., the thought which obliged the truest form of the teachings of Jesus, namely, self denial and love. In this self denial Nietzsche was seeding his possibility for the acquisition of Truth and Knowledge.

Now the formula, faith precedes works, is the great secret found in Nietzsche, this being a faith that was equal to freedom and was not based on belief. I recall Jean-Paul Sartre saying, despite his atheism, that the death of faith in a person creates a "God-shaped-hole" in the soul, but the irony here is that he also felt that because a belief in God destroyed freedom, he must reject God, whether God existed or not. Nietzsche felt the same way, and it eventually led to his mental collapse. When Nietzsche was already close to insanity, in his rejection of God, he called himself the Antichrist. (Jerry, as you and I discussed, both men failed in their attempt to transcend themselves). Nietzsche lacked a true faith, unlike the faith proffered by Luther, a faith that was a lie according to Nietzsche. Nietzsche sought a Faith that drives toward, and embraces, Truth, and then because this Faith is sincere, it even doubts the concept of Truth, leaving Truth only in the arena of probability; adding that, according to Nietzsche, whenever such a faith is so strong and prominently displayed and "makes blessed," it raises suspicion against that which is believed; it does not establish truth, it establishes a certain probability of deception. This kind of faith is binding and shackles the freeness of spirit says Nietzsche (*GM* 148). Real faith is not belief, rather, in the German meaning of faith, it is unconditional, and it never gives up questioning, in fact, not to tremble with the craving and the joy of questioning is contemptible and not true faith. So for Nietzsche the antithesis of faith is to have faith in a 'beautiful sentiment' expressed in Christianity without embracing the deepest innermost need to question it. This course of active faith reflects the guise of freedom independent of compulsion, and yet, *does not exclude* the "make blessed" component for Nietzsche.

Faith is brutal for him, and upon its acquisition, demands of one a serious call to a devout and abstemious life; life as it was is no more; this new man, in erasing the shackles of his past conditioning, must now reach higher and higher and ever more into the incomprehensible; this Nietzsche knew (all excuses for laziness-sloth are now eliminated); but he could not stand it. This type of faith requires a complete renunciation of any interpretation of texts that utilizes "Forcing, adjusting, abbreviating, omitting, padding, inventing, falsifying...; all this expresses, broadly speaking, as much ascetic virtue as any denial of sensuality (it is at bottom only a particular mode of this denial). That which constrains these men, however, **this unconditional will to truth, is faith in the ascetic ideal itself....**" (*On the Genealogy of Morals*, 151). Herein we find that with mental shackles absent, a groundless freedom emerges, a freedom to interpret impartially; indeed, a type of freedom we find in Dostoevsky's novel, *Brothers Karamazov*, where we learn in one scene that the Grand Inquisitor (symbol of darkness in the novel) manages to put the figure of Jesus in jail because he was preaching truth. Well, the Grand Inquisitor tells Jesus that he could convert the townspeople instantly if He wanted to by simply performing one of his miracles, and wondered why He would not do so. Jesus informed the Inquisitor that He wants people to believe in Him **freely**, without any condition, without any coercion or forced influence; this way He knew their Faith in Him would be true.

Human freedom was a very important element in Eastern Christian Orthodoxy, the religion of Dostoevsky who would often seek spiritual guidance from Father Ambrose at the local monastery. Nietzsche admired Dostoevsky's work, and having read his *Notes from the Underground, The House of the Dead, The Injured and Insulted, and I think* Crime and Punishment, never did read *Brothers Karamazov* because it was not translated into French until 1888, in a mutilated version. This fact notwithstanding, I suggest Nietzsche acquired his initial idea about freedom from Christian Orthodox studies and not from a specialized group of Christian Crusaders (monks) in the Orient called the Assassins. These Assassins, informs Nietzsche, epitomized "The "free spirit" image since the watchword for their highest ranks alone was "Nothing is true, everything is permitted." "Very well, that was freedom of spirit; in that way the faith in truth was abrogated" (*On the Genealogy of Morals*, 150). Nietzsche scholar, Walter Kaufmann, informs us that this compelling slogan is not a Nietzschean motto, and was used by him only as a contrast with the unquestioning faith in the truth that characterizes so many so-called free spirits. I agree. Indeed, to not question truth is completely anathema to Nietzsche's idea of freedom; that is, one must be free to question truth, for an unquestioned Truth cannot lead to True Faith, a Faith that has not been honed; a Faith which is not a household god; that is, a god which has produced for Nietzsche a degenerated religion foiled in hypocrisy, falsity, illusions of hell, and sin, and destroyer of human freedom, an observation he held that he hoped could be corrected in time by those two laboring exemplars of philosophy, Kant and Hegel (*Beyond Good and Evil*, 211), the former bringing the concept of duty to man, and Hegel bringing traditional Christianity back into the modern world. It appears many of Nietzsche's ideas came from Hegel, especially his ideas of history and how it can cause harm to religion; the need to return to orthodoxy; the separation of Jesus from the religion He created; and Hegel urged a virtue grounded on authority but a free virtue. These are some of the main similarities between Hegel and Nietzsche and I suspect very surprising to many who might think Nietzsche and Hegel were philosophers exclusively. Hegel has extensive theological writings that Nietzsche, I opine, hoped would gain in popularity so as to accomplish the task he longed for. Recall that Tolstoy's main problem with Christianity was that the religion that emerged from Jesus was unlike his ascetic teachings grounded in unconditional love; a moral objective love neatly articulated by master logician, Immanuel Kant, astutely recognized by Nietzsche.

In addition to Hegel and Kant, Nietzsche had hoped his creation of *Thus Spake Zarathustra* would help enlighten people about the ideal man, the Superman exemplified by Zarathustra. This is the man of **Great Healthiness** as he expresses in the fifth book of *Gay Science*: ..."wants to know how it feels to be the conqueror, and discoverer of the ideal-as likewise how it is with the artist, the saint, the legislator, the sage, the scholar, the devotee, the prophet, and the godly nonconforming of the old style:-requires one thing above all for that great purpose, *great healthiness*...."

In Zarathustra Nietzsche finds it to be his most personal work, a work that personifies his measure of the Dionysian ideal; he being a confessed follower of Dionysos, the epitome of indestructible life, the sensuous Greek God originating in the Minoan culture making its transition to a cosmic religion under the Roman Empire; the latter fact accounting, I suggest, for the reason why Nietzsche found Petronius (d.c.66AD), the Roman satirist and courtier under the Roman Emperor, Claudius Nero (37-68 AD), to exert the strongest influence on him, especially his bawdy novel, *Satyricon*, that gives a vivid portrait of the seamy side of Roman life. A curious fact I will interject regarding Nero and Petronius (before elaborating on Dionysos) is that Petronius was ordered to commit suicide by Nero of which he did. Even more interesting however, is that Nero, referred to as the Caesar to whom St. Paul appealed, and according to substantial tradition, St. Paul and Peter were executed under his reign using them (since they were representatives of Christianity) as scapegoats for a fire that he caused which destroyed most of Rome in 64 AD.

In *Daniel* 3 we learn that cultic statues of the Roman Emperors portray images of the beast, the antichrist (this is the second beast in the 13th chapter of *Revelations*), and this beast is actually a person: "This calls for wisdom: Let anyone with understanding calculate the number of the beast, for it is the number of a person. Its number is six hundred sixty-six" (*Rev.* 13:18). It is calculated that this number is a code based on the numeric value of letters. Well, six hundred sixty-six calculates out from Greek into Hebrew to the numeric value of the name Nero Caesar; this 666 means the epitome of created inadequacy. The numeric value transliterated from Latin into Hebrew is 616. If John was referring to Domitian, whom some considered to be the reincarnation of Nero, it would be safer to not refer to the present persecutor but to the one long gone, or Nero. Some scholars say that John was intentionally enigmatic, using a code to protect against any rebellion directed at government authorities. Now the numeric value of Jesus is 888 meaning on the eighth day (not seventh) Sunday, the day of the Resurrection, the final establishment of God's Kingdom. Eight also means eschatological perfection, a superabundance of fullness. The Holy Trinity is the 777 numeric value. I only show these three sets of numeric values to qualify a pattern intended by John, the inspired writer of *Revelations*, and thus embellish the significance of the *666* numeric allocation to Nero. According to my extensive research on the potency of Hebrew letters (my, *Can Man Influence God* book informs of this), unlike that found in any other language, I find this discovery illuminating. So here we have a possible antichrist figure in Nero killing Petronius, who turns out to be the most important influence in Nietzsche's life, he being the personification of freedom: "Of all books, one of my strongest impressions is that exuberant provencal, Petronius, who composed the last *Satura Menipea [Satyricon]*. Such sovereign freedom from morality, from seriousness, from his own sublime taste; such subtlety in his mixture of vulgar and educated Latin; such indomitable good spirits that leap with grace and malice over all anomalies of the ancient soul. I could not name any book that makes an equally liberating impression on me: the effect is Dionysian. In cases in which I find it necessary to recuperate from a base impression; for example, because for the sake of my critique of Christianity I had to breathe all too long the swampy air of the apostle Paul-a few pages of Petronius suffice me as a heroic remedy, and immediately I am well again" (*Part of a discarded draft for section 3 of "Why I Am So Clever," 236*). I find this history provocative when we consider that Nietzsche, just prior to his death (some claim suicide, his sister claims exhaustion from introspection and a hereditary sickness-she took him in her care the last three years of his life after him being in a mental institution), proclaimed he was the antichrist, as bible scholars claim Nero was, he being the one Petronius sought favor with; and Nietzsche the one who found solace in Petronius; moreover, the one who executed Paul, the very person Nietzsche needed mental respite from. Jerry, I have not found anyone else to have made this curious connection.

Now back to Dionysos. According to Christian Apologist Athenagoras (sec. cent, c.e.), an Apologist who sought to rebut certain false statements against the Christians, namely atheism, describes the birth of Dionysos as follows: "Since his mother Rhea forbade the marriage he desired [Zeus with Rhea], he pursued her. After she had turned herself into a serpent, he did likewise and, entwining her in a so-called Herakleotic knot, entered into union with her. The sign of this form of union is the staff of Hermes. Afterward he entered into union with their daughter Persephone [daughter of Zeus and Rhea] by taking the form of a serpent and raping her. She bore him Dionysos" (*Dionysos, Archetypical Image of Indestructible Life*, Carl Kerenyi, 112). Now the reason why Athenagoras and other Christians, namely Diagoras, were accused of atheism is because Diagoras divulged the Orphic doctrine, and published the Mysteries of Eleusis. It is believed that the Orphic Mysteries (which probably evolved from Pythagoras due to their similarities in my opinion, especially their strict adherence to self discipline and ascetic practices) became associated with the myth of Dionysos due to the parallels evident in their stories. We first learn of a central motif in their stories when, in prehistoric times, a young male was ritually sacrificed by being cut into pieces, and while lacking archaeological evidence, these pieces of flesh were then planted into the ground to please the Orphic powers (powers that inhabit the underworld), and thus ensure abundant crops. In Orphic doctrine, Hades (the underworld) is the place of regeneration and eventual rebirth. Using these Orphic powers, Orpheus, and those schooled in the Mysteries of the occult, could provide spiritual guidance as a means of expiating guilt and prepare the soul for the afterlife. And, like we find in Christianity, souls who were cleansed of their sins and who had been initiated into the Orphic Mysteries, could expect to be reborn in new bodies to renew their quest for true purity and eventual escape from the wheel of reincarnation much like you find in Buddhism or Hinduism. It has been said that the Orphic doctrine is probably more Buddhist, but it has numerous Hindu parallels, and some Christian ones as well, especially the parable of the Vine that I will discuss later. I should add at this point that several versions of Hades (underworld) has been portrayed by poets over the centuries. In the Hebrew scriptures we find a similarly dark view of the underworld, wherein one can find the good and bad souls housed in an underground region called Sheol, very similar to what is found in Homer's version of Hades.

    Mystics attracted to Orphism sought to create a variation of the Dionysian myth and created a different version of Dionysos's double birth which would more closely connect this god of wine to the regenerative powers of the Underworld. (Recall Nietzsche saying that one of the beauties of religion is that it can alter its myth). Now according to Orphic teachings, Dionysos is originally the son of Zeus and Persephone. Well, Zeus plans to enthrone his divine son as king of the universe by combining his celestial power with Orphic wisdom. The ever-jealous Hera, however, induces the Titans to kill Dionysos by tearing him into pieces and boiled them in water before roasting them, and while tasting these pieces of flesh, Jupiter, roused by the odor and perceiving the cruelty of the deed, hurled his thunder (god of thunder) at the Titans; and committed the pieces of Dionysos (Bacchus) to Apollo, his brother, that they might be properly interred. Acting for her father, Athene manages to save the child's heart, which she gives to Zeus, who swallows it, and then impregnates Semele. The son of Zeus and Persephone, re-formed in Semele's womb, is reborn Dionysos Zagreus. Through this birthing process of Dionysos, Orphism teaches that humans house a dual nature, i.e., the evil impulses of Titans, and the spark of divinity in the form of Dionysos's body. Because of this spark of divinity within, all humans can potentially awaken to their god within, but only through ritual purification and a communal meal of wine and flesh; something like is found in the Christian communion with wine and a wafer symbolic of the flesh of Christ. As we find in Pythagoras and later Plato, the body is viewed, in these coordinated myths, as the prison of the soul (sema) 114–115 Carl Kerenyi).

Like Christianity, we find miracles performed by Dionysos. One in particular has him, while posing as a young boy, being kidnapped by pirates and held for ransom. When the sailors fail to recognize his divinity, Dionysos changes these pirates into dolphins and causes a massive vine, bearing huge clusters of grapes, to grow over the pirates' ship. Dionysos' divinity is thus revealed in natural phenomena-the vine sprouting miraculously in an unnatural environment. Similarly, in Christianity, Jesus, the Christ, the God He is, is revealed in the natural world, in the flesh. And like I stated much earlier, there are 2,045 plus versions of this Christian story, only a few live on in the Dionysian story.

The religion emerging from Orpheus was a conflation of the orgiastic passion of Dionysos (some secret rituals involved worshippers being initiated into the Dionysian cult witnessing a climactic unveiling of an oversized model of the god's penis as an emblem of divine virility) and the ascetic control of Apollo suggesting the essential unity of these otherwise antithetical forces: In Dionysian lore each person has within them a *potent life-willing force and a potent death or destroying force*, as in the war between emotion and intellect.

Herodotus and Pindar claim that Orpheus was an actual person, but Aristotle was not sure. Although the Orphic teachings are said to originate from Egypt, some say it could have originated from India since it has many parallels to Buddhist doctrines as I mentioned earlier. Also, the Orphic teachings were clearly ascetic, and the Dionysiacal sacred rites revolved around this practice suggesting an origin of Nietzsche's proclivity toward the ascetic ideal. It should be noted that all fables, as in this myth, embrace ceremonies that involve the gods and also the human soul. So, by Dionysos, we are to understand the spiritual part of the mundane soul; for there are various processions or avatars of this god, or Bacchuses, derived from his essence. The Titans (recall they cut Dionysos into pieces) represent the mundane gods of whom Bacchus is the highest. The cunning tactics employed by the Titans, in order to ensnare Dionysos, are symbolical of the divisible operations of these mundane gods seeking to tear into pieces Dionysos's intellect to discombobulate him. Jupiter symbolizes the demiurges or god of providence, essence and power, or artificer of the universe, and Apollo symbolizes the deity of the Sun, who has both a mundane and super-mundane quality, and by whom the universe is bound in symmetry and consent.

Dionysos is the guardian of generation because he presides over life and death (recall his birth process); he is the guardian over life because of generation, and guardian over death because wine produces an enthusiastic condition, both eruptive and irruptive. In his attempt to live out the Dionysian spirit of a divided, or scattered intellect endeavoring to rejoin the pieces of his intellect to matter, to their source from hence they came, Nietzsche chose the eruptive path indicated by his profoundly expressive and exaggerated contrapuntal language. In this process of intellect dispersion and illumination from higher reason, even though this process proceeds into the dark and rebounding receptacle of matter, its heretofore obscurity is invested with the supervening ornaments of divine light, erewhile returning at the same time, that is, without interruption, to the source of its descent. In this we can see how he embodies the subconscious and instinctive life force that animates nature. Because he is the god of wine, and therefore, the provider of intoxication, he shatters conventional restraints and permits humans to act out extremes of emotion and behavior. This Nietzsche did without reticence because he knew that in order to give birth to the divine god within he had to be totally immersed in its opposite, and literally become a Titan or apostate (one who forsakes their religion or cause), in order to realize a higher potential, for him that is the Ubermensch or Superman represented in his novel *Thus Spake Zarathustra*, a story we discussed at length in the seventies. When he proclaimed he was an atheist (an apostate actually) he was performing, in my opinion, his own intra-personal Sacred rite in the name of his mentor, Dionysos, knowing full well that his brother, Apollo, being the deity of purification in the myth, and his true savior, would rescue him from the revolving wheel of dark Titan energy: alas, Dionysos is rested from his labors (ascetic) purifying himself from the contamination of earthly life, and therefore, is freed from his bondage to the body, and thus departs his apostatizing life. Dionysos is now prepared to reside with the gods: he now lives in, and is subsisted by the sun witnessed by his transport through the heavens in circular motion observed by the Orphic verse titled *Dionysos, Soul of the Sun*: "Dionysos, child of the primal fire,/we honor you./ You are the eye of Kore/watching us/...Golden haired Apollo,/ripen our vines" (*The Hymns of Orpheus*, R.C. Hogart, 118). In another verse we read: "He is called Dionysos, because he is carried with a circular motion through the immensely extended heavens." In Orphic theology the divinity of the **Sun** boasts a mundane (intellectual) as well as a super-mundane, or exalting nature, both which are subsumed by Dionysos.

I have stressed the contrapuntal language of Nietzsche and his intentional play of contradictions throughout his writings; well for initiates in the Orphic-Dionysian tradition, conflict is merely cycle swept away by an inevitable resolution that bridges every contrariety. Harmony always wins. Gurdjieff proclaims loudly that humans are third force blind; this third force is resolution and is in full sight of the Orphic-Dionysos initiate.

We are all a tangled skein with one thread bound by our inner Titan, another by our inner Dionysos. The Titan thread is deceitful, rebellious, violent and mortal, while the Dionysos thread is immortal, wise and serene. Hogart tells us that "We live many lives purging the Titan; as a result the Orphics taught catharsis through a course of abstinence and self discipline replacing drunken frenzy with rites of purification and spiritual enthusiasm and ecstasy: the Orphic enthousiasmos [to have God within] and ekstasis [to stand outside oneself in trance-as in out of body]" (23).

Like Jesus wanted His followers to become, Orpheus was also a Fisherman, the Good Shepherd, the Bridegroom, and like St. Francis of Assisi, was often surrounded by peaceful animals. According to Hobart, Orphism influenced, paralleled, or borrowed from Christianity so profoundly that the nineteenth-century German scholar, Dr. Eisler, insisted Christianity stole the crucifixion from the wheel in the Orphic Mysteries. Orphics were supposed to have been tied to the wheel so they could feel the dizzy helplessness of repeated reincarnation in forgetfulness (24). While Nietzsche says he acquired his idea of eternal recurrence (exact circumstances in life repeat themselves for an eternity) while walking by the seashore, and thereby, infused his *Thus Spake Zarathustra* novel with this most important revelation for him, I suggest he more likely acquired it from his Egyptian studies and early Christianity, possibly provoked by his obvious Dionysian/Orphic knowledge of the ever-spinning wheel of reincarnation which is not the same as eternal recurrence, but the idea bears a resemblance nevertheless, enough to pique one's interest in the concept. For Nietzsche, and his overburdened bouts of loneliness throughout his entire life (he did not have anyone who could understand him), the idea of eternal recurrence was revolting, and I suspect had a lot to do with his mental collapse, not to mention his obsession with, merging with Dionysos in a higher marriage, (all Orphic insights by Hogart).

Because the image of Ariadne played such a major role in Nietzsche's psyche and figured in his mental collapse according to some scholars, I will provide a brief description of her. The name Ariadne is a Cretan-Greek form for Arihagne, meaning the "utterly pure." Her name actually is more an epithet, an expression of her attributes. She was the daughter of the evil-plotting Minos, an epithet that presupposes the labyrinth (underworld) as a place of death. From Homer we learn that she is described as the girl "with beautiful braids of hair," an ornamental epithet that Homer confers more often on goddesses than on common girls. Her especial qualities are first recognized when she is credited with saving Theseus, her lover, from the labyrinth by using a magical thread made famous by Homer and embellished by Sophocles. In the Athenian view it was actually Aphrodite who helped Theseus out of the labyrinth, but it's also possible, according to this story, that Aphrodite guided Ariadne by her (Aphrodite's) power, or the hero could have simply met the goddess embodied in Aphrodite's daughter suggesting Ariadne could have been a mortal Aphrodite who dies with her unborn child in the underworld, hence the derivation of her being called the mistress of the labyrinth (underworld). While this humanizes the myth informs Carl Kerenyi, in his book, *Dionysos*, it did become a realistic invention that has become a cult legend, a legend Nietzsche was well aware of, and his query "Who knows...what Ariadne is," is made more explicable when we learn from Kerenyi, that Ariadne not only mirrored the Great Goddesses like Artemis (goddess of virginity), Aphrodite (goddess of love), and Persephone (goddess of underworld who let Orpheus take his wife back to earth-he being one of the few mortals to have ever returned from the underworld); Ariadne was also Persephone and Ariadne in one person! It may also be assumed that she gave birth in the underworld.

Nietzsche may well have longed for her to invade his being likewise, and lift him out of his hellish labyrinth; his obsession with her and her mate Dionysos, suggests the plausibility of this idea. Moreover, her immortality is announced by Hesiod (born sometime around the second half of the eighth century and the first quarter of the seventh century b.c.e.) in Theogony:....: "Golden-Haired Dionysos took blond Ariadne,/ daughter of Minos, to be his buxom bride,/ and then Zeus made her ageless and immortal" (*Hesiod, Theogony, Works and Days, Shield*, Apostolos N. Athanassakis, Ins. 947-49). The scene of the marriage was in the Aegean Sea on the small island of Donus or Donusia, east of Naxos. Interestingly, the huge marble frame of the gate erected for Dionysos on the site of the *Sacred Marriage* is still standing to this day. This type of setting, says Kerenyi, is characteristic not only of the Minoan religion, but also the prehistoric religion of the entire island world.

I opened this discussion of Ariadne with the statement that Dionysos and Ariadne would evolve into a higher marriage. This idea can be seen when we consider that just as Dionysos is the archetypical reality of *zoe* (lover of life and nature), so Ariadne is the archetypical reality of the bestowal of soul, or that which individuates a human, a key idea for Nietzsche. The soul is an essential element of zoe, which needs it to transcend limitations imposed by its inherent affinity for life-nature. In this symbiosis and reciprocal feeding of mental influences, zoe's conception in soul is assured with woman as provider. With the reflection of this impregnating image being the **moon**, the mythological seat of the soul is revealed. (Recall that Dionysos is the image of the Sun, his home; so we can now see an evolving conflation between the Moon and Sun in this myth). In the union of these two archetypical images, the divine couple, Dionysos and Ariadne, represent the eternal passage of zoe into and through the genesis of living creatures, and Dionysos, as the carrier of the vessel, rides heavenward with Ariadne while the cosmos literally unfolds before their eyes, and surrounded in the outermost zone of the zodiac, Ariadne sets her jeweled crown in the sky as a constellation. I suggest this constellation could be either capricorn or cancer, both of which are described as the celestial gateways according to Greek astronomy; that is, gateways where the soul exits earth into the next world. (Jerry, I will provide you a map showing the exact coordinate/degree location of these gateways). Now whether it be the Greek religion or the Minoan religion, this process occurs over and over again, and is always, uninterruptedly, present. Not only in the Greek religion, but also in the earlier Minoan religion and mythology, zoe takes the masculine form [recall Dionysos is carrier of this form], while the genesis of souls takes the feminine form, in this case, Ariadne! We learn from Kerenyi that in this process the **mystery of death** is revealed as a **mystery of enhanced life** in a divine marriage [*of opposites*] (373).

Recall that in the asceticism conveyed by Nietzsche that by destroying the passions (as in die to passions) one gives life to the inner garden of soul, a special joy emerges, the seed for the Ubermensch is planted; the womb for Ariadne is ready for her invasion. In this we find Nietzsche acquiescing to the Dionysian ideal (Nietzsche himself acting the part of Dionysos), and his longing for Ariadne increases in proportion to his developing into the

Superman, the apostate who has sacrificed his heritage to attract the favor of Ariadne. I suggest that by Nietzsche emphasizing the This-Worldly aspect in his philosophy, he was either inadvertently, or intentionally, seeking to manifest the third rung in the critical cosmological *Law of Three*, namely, the force of the Sun, being the positive life giving force (Dionysos-zoe); the force of the Moon (gravitational-dark-underworld; Ariadne was/is goddess of the Moon and mistress of the underworld), and the earth, the neutralizing medium through which the divine pair can resolve their opposite forces into a unity; a divine marriage. In this story, as in the Jesus story, a key component is that the central figures become human, that is, **earthbound**: Upon discovering the secret of growing grapes, Dionysos wandered far and wide teaching his art of the intoxicating pleasures of wine that inspired wild dances of ecstasy as they celebrated their liberation. Now in Nietzsche's self destructing and persistent contrapuntal passages where one passage can destroy the one before it, as in contradiction, his ascetic ideal to controvert the passions and reuse them for higher expressions to self-create a Superman to escape a version of life that he actually saw as death to higher values, his penchant to destroy customary values wrapped in artifice espoused by insincere, phony men, and finally, in his confessed atheism (his symbolic gesture toward an inner death I suggest) after his announcement that God is dead years before, do we not find a man fulfilling his perception of the Dionysian ideal?!

While often times Nietzsche can be seen espousing a polemic regarding the passions in order to make fun of, or simply excoriate the church and its phony soldiers, especially the Lutheran-Protestant breed, so commonly evident in *The Genealogy of Morals*, which is why, by the way, understanding the context in which he writes is crucial to comprehending his contrariety; in one of his very last books, *Twilight of the Idols*, written in 1888 and published in 1889, he writes in straight forward prose the following:

To exterminate the passions and desires merely in order to do away with their folly and its unpleasant consequences-this itself seems to us today merely an acute form of folly...On the soil out of which Christianity grew the concept '*spiritualization* of passion' could not possibly be conceived. For the primitive Church, as is well known, fought against the 'intelligent' in favor of the 'poor in spirit': how could one expect from it an intelligent war against passion? The church combats the passions with excision in every sense of the word: its practice, its 'cure' is castration. It never asks how can one spiritualize, beautify, deify a desire? It has at all times laid the emphasis of its discipline on extirpation. But to attack the passions at their roots means to attack life at its roots: the practice of the Church is hostile to life.... chap: *Morality as Anti-Nature*, (1).

What Nietzsche means by spiritualizing the passions is sublimating, and transforming the beastly, animal energy of the body, into a higher, that is, spiritual expression. To castrate this sex or chi energy is to destroy one's chances of ever experiencing spiritual transformation. I wrote in my *Single Eye of Light* book that, in accordance with the teachings of the Holy Fathers of the Eastern Orthodox Church, if a person has not experienced an enlightened spiritual transformation by the age of sixty for a male, and fifty-five for a female, then they will have missed out on ever being able to advance spiritually because at these ages one does undergo a symbolic castration of life-sex-chi force. This is simply because the sex drive is diminishing too much. Meaning one needs the evil of the sex drive to experience the godly manifestation of its sublimated result in spiritual expression. The appropriation and exegesis of the particulars in order to execute this holy practice is well known in the Orthodox Church. John Cassian (c.360-after 430), a founder of two monasteries near Marseilles in 415 A.D., who wrote the ordinary rules for the monastic life and reveals the chief hindrances to a monk's perfection (many of which were acquired from his journey to Egypt) that eventually formed the basis of many Western Monastic Rules, had this to say about ascetic practice and a lifeless (or as Nietzsche says-castration) body: "Only the lifeless are exempt from the battles of lust. We know, then, that the struggle of flesh and the spirit is **extremely useful** to us...to gain self-control and mastery over our desires" (*What the Church Fathers Say About...*, George Grube, ed. 68). Regarding the dignity of human life, Church Father, St. Irenaeus (c.130-c.200), had this to say: "The glory of God is a human being who is fully alive, and the life of such a person consists in beholding God" (159).

In light of the necessity to suppress the base passions in order to accomplish perfection as taught in the Ancient Church, and as we find in Nietzsche, monks would channel their base drives in study, copying scriptures over and over, recite prayer, write God pleasing prose or poems, and paint/draw Icons, all in an effort to Spiritualize or transform their lower beastly passions, and self-create an opening for God to live in unencumbered by His hosts' self-willed base drives. These tasks, in the very nature of their transmutation potential, served/serve ascetics well to prevent sitting on a psychological volcano of unused sex-chi energy, e.g., witness bouts of anger, excitability, or any extremes in behavior, especially gluttony, that the Fathers proclaim was/is, among other things, a lust for sexual orgasms. Freud would even agree with the latter: in sexual orgasm ego is momentarily suspended; one is in a state of self-forgetfulness-all problems are extinguished for that moment; a like scenario is also experienced with food consumption. Jerry, even Tolstoy was aware of this need to re-channel sex energy; he stating manual labor was very useful for this purpose. The Holy Fathers require their monks to partake of gardening; this being one of the reasons, that is, to spiritualize the beastly passions.

If Nietzsche's allegation includes all Christian churches, as implied in the above quote, namely, Eastern Orthodoxy, Roman Catholic and the Reformed Churches, I suggest his lack of knowledge of the therapeutic art of ascetic labors within the two former churches is clearly evident. Whether it be Buddhism, Hinduism, Sufism, Taoism, or Eastern Orthodoxy, excising the passions would be profoundly antithetical to the goals of these respective monks, which is to bring life to an otherwise dead body smothered and consumed by the animal passions. This process cannot occur without the God-given beastly energy, a concept characteristic of all these traditions.

In deference to Nietzsche, I must add that translations of the teachings of the Greek and Russian Fathers of the Eastern Orthodox Church were sparse during his time, and therefore, might lead him to render a generalized critique possibly projecting what he saw in the Lutheran-Protestant Reformed movement. Nietzsche did know of Calvin though, and it was Calvin who sought to bring the teachings of the Fathers of the Eastern Orthodox Church to the mainstream; this he did but their (Fathers) emphasis on asceticism turned many of the blind faith followers away who preferred the easy, just claim you are a believer way, to the struggles of true religious practice espoused by the above listed traditions. Because Nietzsche did make numerous praiseworthy references to the early church practices of true religion in his early writings (I provided quotes from some) all of which included, according to his sister in her *Preface* to his collected writings, foreshadows of his ideal man, the Ubermenche, the Superman in Zarathustra, I'm inclined to surmise that Nietzsche was referencing the Lutheran-Protestant churches in this quote. Moreover, in his *Notes* that were published posthumously, of which I have provided several quotes from, his sister saying they were all notes for his last book, *The Will to Power*, and was to serve as a culmination of his work, and unfortunately, dying before completing it, I'm inclined the more to think he was only referring to the Lutheran, Protestant and Catholic churches, despite his mention of the primitive church. But then to allege Nietzsche is being inconsistent here is comical, since that is his specialty anyway, a specialty that contrives to avoid any pattern in his thought process to prevent anyone from developing a Nietzschean system; after all, for him, to have a system is to neuter the nexus that grins in the face of his Freedom theme so beautifully endemic to this Orphic/Dionysian Fragment that he had to be familiar with, in fact, probably fired his passion for Dionysos:

> From planet to planet we fall,
> crying for home in the abyss,
> we are your tears Dionysos.
>
> Mighty One! **God of Freedom**!
> Bring your children back into
> your heart of singing light (*The Hymns of Orpheus, 31*).

Herodotus, born in 485 b.c.e., and the Father of History and Ethnography, reports in his *Histories*, a curious fact about the Scythians who learned that a dire fate awaits those who adopt customs imported from anyone else, especially Greeks. Without getting into details, Scyles, one of the sons of King Ariapithes of Scythia, was destined for a bad end when he sought to perform the Bacchic-Dionysian rites. Just as he was about to do the rite, a tremendous omen occurred. Zeus struck his luxurious house in the Borysthenite community with a bolt of lightening and it burnt to the ground. Now after Scyles had performed these Bacchic Dionysian rites, one of the Borysthenites hurried off to the Scythians and said, "You may mock our Bacchic-Dionysian rites, men of Scythia, and the fact that the god takes hold of us, but now the god has taken hold of your own king, and he is in a state of Bacchi-Dionysian frenzy. If you don't believe me, come and I will show you." When the sacred procession went past the building, with Scyles in it, they could see that he was possessed by Dionysos. They thought this was a disaster. From this incident, reports Herodotus, the Scythians learned "that it was unreasonable to seek out a god [in this case, Dionysos], who drives people out of their minds" (Book Four, 259-62). Once Scyles' people discovered his initiation, they revolted and kill him. There are other similar incidents provided by Herodotus of dire fates to people who embrace foreign religious rites. The moral here is that one should not adopt customs imported from anyone else, especially the Greeks. Ancient history historian, Thomas Harrison, reports in *Divinity and History*, a similar prognosis stating: "The belief in the identity of one's own and others' gods is all very well in theory, but not in practice. When foreigners do attempt to propitiate Greek gods, it is frequently the case that no good comes of it" (217). Well, the whole world knows what happened to Nietzsche, he too, a non-Greek, went out of his mind in his maddening search for not only Dionysos, but his mate, Ariadne!!! Maybe the problem for both, in addition to what I just conveyed, is that they never found Ariadne to balance the Dionysian force of the Sun, an obsessive quandary that proved a major problem for Nietzsche.

One more point on the Dionysos theme and its connection to the vineyard. When Jesus journeyed during his public ministry to the region of Tyre and Sidon, the farthest beyond Israel, He observed wine growers, and as a result culled many of his metaphors from their lives, as did the poets and prophets of the Old Testament before Him. When Jesus proclaims "I am the true Vine, and my father is the wine dresser" (*John* 15:1), He is recalling His journey to this region, a region that some say is where He noticed the occurrence of a massive Dionysian religion. Two of the most important places in the Old Testament in which the vine is used as a symbol are found in Jeremiah and Isaiah. In response to the ritual prostitution of Canaanite and Phoenician fertility cults, in *Jeremiah* 2:20-21, we read "But I have taken no joy in you," says the Lord your God, "for from of old [could this be an allusion to Dionysos' religion?] you have splintered your yoke and have broken your chain to pieces [recall that part of the Dionysian sacrificial rite is to break-tear into pieces the flesh of an animal, or in the case of Dionysos, he was broken into pieces with only his heart being preserved]. You have said, I will not serve You, but I will go to every high hill and under every shade tree to indulge in my fornication. I planted a fruitful vine for you, one most healthy and sweet, yet you turned it into a vine unknown to me, with a taste of bitterness." In *Isaiah* 1:4 we read: "But now I tell you what shall I do to my vineyard that I have not done for it? For I waited for it to bring forth grapes, but it produced thorn plants." Noteworthy, but not surprisingly, is that in the Old Testament images of Jesus in the Old Testament, Jesus is the planter of the vine and informs of a healthy fruit to come, whereas, in the New Testament of *John* 15:1, Jesus, or God Himself, is not the planter of the vine, but is the vine Himself. However, it is not until we get to the *Song of Solomon* in the Old Testament that we find a closer alignment to the Dionysian theme of Ariadne and Dionysos united in a mystical marriage. We learn that the lover likens her lover to a vineyard, "My own vineyard is before me"(8:12), which is the bride telling Solomon, owner of many vineyards, and symbolic of the Holy Church or Christ, that she now has another vineyard to tend, her husband, the inner vineyard, wherein, she is inviting her husband to ascend into heaven to enjoy His victories, while she continues working for His glory and the spread of His kingdom on earth. The Groom responds, "You who dwells in the gardens"(8:13), professing a prophetic gesture of encouragement of the Ascension, after which Christ will come again to receive us to Himself (*Jn* 14:3). When Nietzsche proclaimed "Who knows...what Ariadne is," he implied not only his longing for her, his inner bride, but his inner torment over his **individuation**, his singleness, his exclusive Dionysian embrace minus the Other. Furthermore, when Nietzsche uttered "Who was that, What was that," in response to Jesus dying on the Cross, he shared the following sentiment: "the exemplary element in his manner of dying, the freedom from, the superiority over every feeling of resentment-a sign of how little they understood him at all....For the Evangel had been precisely the existence, the fulfillment, the actuality of this kingdom. Such a death was precisely this kingdom of God..." (*The Antichrist, 40*). Nietzsche saw the death of Jesus as His way of bringing the kingdom of God to us now, and by He not feeling any resentment, demonstrated the Evangel spirit in the highest degree, the very antithesis to what evolved, or was intended from this incident, according to Nietzsche, which was/is revengefulness, retribution and punishment all awaiting judgment; the seed for this scenario, he adds, was Paul, whom he says also did not reveal the precise teachings of Jesus. Imagine Jerry, the aforementioned was in Nietzsche's book, *The Antichrist*, suggestive precisely that his angst was not over Jesus Himself, but what ideas emanated from Him. Now this kingdom of God is the interior vineyard that needs constant pruning, as in crossing out excess, according to Nietzsche (this I illustrated earlier) and the Holy Fathers, to stem the current of bestial passions; well, I suggest that just as Jesus is the symbolic pruning shear for a Christian, so was Ariadne Nietzsche's anticipated pruning shear, a figure he never experienced consummation with, or did he? His equivalent uttered words on both her account and Jesus' were incomplete. So we can surmise from this postulate that his interior vineyard needs a nurturing only she can provide, as a Christian needs Christ to nurture and render him/herself complete *again*. Perhaps, what Ariadne is to the Dionysian story, the Blessed Virgin Mary (the *Theotokos*) is to the Christian story; or in Dante's case, Beatrice; or in Virgil's case, Dido!!

In the Dionysian story we learn that proper worship of him can not only save one from the Fates (the three goddesses-sisters-Clotho, Lachesis and Atropos who decide the fate of all humans, and some say, even the destiny of the gods themselves) imposed by the cosmos, but also a blessed afterlife is assured where one can continue their sensuous indulgences as some scholars imply. I suggest that the sensuality implied is not of a lewd nature because in Euripides' play, *The Bacchae*, it being a central source of Dionysian knowledge, the Chorus, in observing Dionysos going to the holy mountain, utters the following words:

> Blest is the happy man
> Who knows the mysteries of the gods ordain,
> And sanctifies his life,
> Joins soul with soul in mystic unity,
> And, by due ritual made pure,
> Enters the ecstasy of mountain solitude;
> Who observes the mystic rites
> Made lawful Cybele the Great Mother;
> Who crowns his head with ivy [emblem of Dionysos],
> And shakes aloft his wand in worship of Dionysos (194).

A few lines forward we read of Dionysos' admonition to chastity:

> ...Dionysos will not compel
> Women to be chaste, since in all matters of self control
> Resides in our own natures. You should consider this;
> For in Bacchic ritual, as elsewhere, a woman
> Will be safe from corruption if her mind is chaste (202).

Jerry, if you reread my chapter on *The Three Forms of Sexual Attraction*, in the *Moments...* book, you will see a description of this mystical union or intercourse, wherein the etheric bodies merge to one complete form, since the flesh is out of the way to impede full penetration of one complete body into another; and this is done without orgasm. I know it's common knowledge to associate Dionysos with lasciviousness, but as you can see from Euripides, the deeper significance of Dionysos is more correctly aligned with purity. I believe Nietzsche also saw Dionysos in a more esoteric, deeper way. Euripides seems to be intimating the same thing when he shows Dionysos' anger over some characters in the play accusing his mother of being born of a non-virgin birth, and even of him not being a god (192-94). This could be however, Euripides' injecting his own views of virginity into the play. Also, regarding Nietzsche's marriage to Ariadne, a few opinions surface: Dionysos seduces Ariadne, then Theseus (her lover) carries her off and Dionysos prevails on Artemis (goddess of chastity) to kill her; Theseus and/or Dionysos seduce her, and Artemis kills Ariadne for unchastity; Or Dionysos marries her. Dominant scholarship, based on Hesiod's *Theogony*, have Dionysos marrying Ariadne at the end of *Theogony*, and as a result, Zeus, the father of Dionysos, makes Ariadne immortal: "And then Zeus made her ageless and immortal" (949). And because Dionysos and Ariadne appear together so frequently in vase paintings (recall that paintings are one way for determining origins of religions), it has been established that Dionysos and Ariadne simply got married without any lewd particulars. We also learn in the Theogony that Dionysos and Ariadne do not have any children, in fact, this god of wine never gave birth to any children according to all archaic sources. As we find in one version of the Dionysian story, we have also found in the Jesus story: Jesus and Mary Magdalene as a married couple. Recall that in one of my letters to you over two years ago, I responded to your query about the famous, so called kiss between Mary and Jesus, as being merely His way of infusing His breath into her, and not to embrace her in the classic sensuous manner; I used Hebraic philology to demonstrate my point, in addition to verses culled from the *Gospel of Philip* itself.

In his *The Birth of Tragedy*, wherein Nietzsche expounds his premise that all early Greek Tragedy was about the sufferings and glorification of Dionysian chorus confluent with, and enhanced by the Apollonian image (recall that Apollo is Dionysos' brother in the myth's story), his balancing agent that forged interior unification, we learn of his prolific words that lament his divorce from unity and subsequent pessimistic view of the world: "...Together with the *mystery doctrine of tragedy*: the fundamental knowledge of the oneness of everything existent, the concept of **individuation** as the prime cause of evil, and of art as the joyous hope that the bonds of individuation may be broken in augury of restored oneness" (231). In describing Aeschylus' tragedy, *Prometheus*, a tragedy that revolved around the symbiotic union of Dionysos and Apollo, Nietzsche observes that it was the Heracleian (Hercules) power of music that freed Prometheus from his vultures, and thus transformed the myth into a vehicle of Dionysian wisdom. And this occurred, he adds, because music invests myths with a new and most profound significance (232). Through this investment of added power to myth with music, an aura of invincibility is added to the story (witness Christian and Indian, especially Buddhist music, for example), and, says Nietzsche, "...they tremble under the piercing glance of this goddess-till the powerful fist of the Dionysian artist forces them into the service of a new deity" (232). Because the Greeks owned a total perception of the essence of Dionysos, they did not require an intellectual formulation of him, and subsequently, like Nietzsche, were joyous over the energy his image produced: the intention of Dionysian worship was to ingest the intoxicating power of the god and to exhibit divine possession; in fact, even eating the raw flesh of an animal as a way of feeding on the Dionysian power in the animal that in addition to inspiring ecstasy, also created madness/insanity. While Nietzsche is not referencing Ariadne at this point, his unconscious could be, because, like I said earlier, according to Nietzsche scholars, his obsession with her image contributed largely to his mental collapse.

    Noteworthy however, is that the stronghold, vitality and continuity of this mythic manifestation is jeopardized once we subject the myth to what Nietzsche calls historico-pragmatical *juvenile his-*

tory, and the very myths that spark and fuel the feeling associated with the religion, perishes leaving in its wake a dried out religion smothered to death by its historical foundation (*The Birth of Tragedy*, 232). Referencing both Hegel and Nietzsche earlier, I espoused briefly their expanded views on the harm historical exegesis presents to religion, that is, the idea that over-analysis of a myth jeopardizes its purpose to seed the transport of the imagination into the metaphysical; the metaphysical that ignites the Active Imagination to carry the soul away from its body. Nietzsche describes how modernizing the original Greek tragedies, through over-systematizing their Dionysian origins, has diminished their ability to inspire awe and wonder. Joseph Campbell, in his attempt to render a modernized interpretation of various details contained within the myth, as I demonstrated earlier, had the same negative effect, only from a different angle. Obviously, both Nietzsche and Hegel were traditionalists, each sought to not disassemble the parts of *The Mysteries*, rather, cull from them what divine wonders they can provide: this, a well fed Active Imagination is Free! to do. Intellectualization destroys many things, but its greatest victim is the Freedom to create; in this regard, Nietzsche would add, to create a destiny with Ariadne; Sartre would say, to create himself; Gurdjieff would say, to create a Soul. Ironically, as famously empirically minded as John Locke was, he still embraced the idea of Christianity, the Mystery of the Trinity, et cetera; in fact, creating a book titled, "*The Reasonableness of Christianity*."

Keeping within the authors I discussed in this letter, so disturbed was Tolstoy and Nietzsche over the fact that the teachings of the original Jesus did not reflect what He in fact taught or represented, the former had to create an entire book, "*The Gospel in Brief*," to inform the public in easy language what He really taught, and the latter, in proclaiming he was the Antichrist, merely cast forth a rebellious statement affirming his perturbation over the reality of the same problem. In both cases, these authors saw the original story so contrived, so melted down over time, that the first seed of the story was no more; Where did Jesus go; He is no more. When Nietzsche uttered "Who is Ariadne," could he have been alluding to this very destruction of the primal seed? Maybe she too, was over analyzed!

A built in comportment now surfaces that segues ideally with the inhibitory effects of over analysis, pragmatic historicity, and smothered Active Imagination; and that is the concept of Apophaticism, or negative theology, a concept I cover in depth in my book, *Can Man Influence God?* First and foremost is that negative theology is a very important idea found in Eastern Christian Orthodoxy. Apophaticism can be likened to sculpting a face. In order to derive a likeness one has to keep peeling away layer upon layer of clay, and though in measured sequences, eventually a likeness is achieved like magic; suddenly a soulful image is materialized. The soul of the person is now revealed. In negative theology the soul peels away all ideas and images of God, shattering all assumptions even, and enters into the darkness that is beyond understanding, and given this nothingness, becomes wholly united with the Ineffable. The transport of this perception becomes the person's affirmation that the essence of God is Unknowable, and one can only know Him through His energies. (Recall how the Greeks thrived off the energy of Dionysos). An expanded view of this Apophaticism is best described by Vladimir Lossky, in his book, *Mystical Theology of the Eastern Church*:

> Negative theology is not merely a theory of ecstasy. It is an expression of that fundamental attitude which transforms the whole of theology into contemplation of the mysteries of revelation. It is not a branch of theology, or chapter, or an inevitable introduction on the incomprehensibility of God from which one passes unruffled to a doctrinal exposition in the usual terminology of human reason and philosophy in

general. Apophaticism teaches us to see above all negative meaning in the dogmas of the Church: it forbids us to follow natural ways of thought and to form concepts which would usurp the place of spiritual realities. For Christianity is not a philosophical school for speculating about abstract concepts, but is essentially a communion with the living God. That is why, despite all their philosophical learning and natural bent towards speculation, the fathers of the eastern tradition, in remaining faithful to the apophatic principle of theology, never allowed their thought to cross the threshold of the **mystery** (my emphasis), or to substitute idols of God for God Himself (42).

In negative theology we must see that it is a way of stripping away all positive opinions or ideas we have about God in order to apprehend a supreme ignorance of Him whom cannot be known. This is a kind of intellectual purification that fuels an intentional turning away from our preconceived notions about God. When Nietzsche praised Christianity, his "God is dead" and "I am the antichrist" proclamations notwithstanding, were his ways of embracing negative theology, either consciously of unconsciously, however maligned it may have appeared on the surface. My premise for this opinion is that no matter how anti-Christian, Buddha, Allah, Krishna, or the Like one becomes, one cannot outrun God who lives in an about all of us, whether we approve or disapprove, not even Nietzsche can run that fast, nor did he want to, and now even Darwin's prized Tree of Life contingency has suffered a major gap making it appear more and more that not even he could out-run God; a finding I'll discuss later.

When Nietzsche declared "God is Dead" he did not mean God never was/is. Rather, as he stated in *The Gay Science*, "God is dead. God remains dead. And we have killed him. How shall we comfort ourselves, the murderers of all murderers? What was *holiest* and mightiest of all that the world has yet owned *has bled to death under our knives*: who will wipe this blood off us.... Is not the greatness of this deed too great for us. Must we ourselves not become gods simply to appear worthy of it....?" (125). In a final edition of *The Gay Science* (1887), Nietzsche adds: ..."the Christian God has become unbelievable...." (sect. 343). Nearing his mental collapse now, in his book, *The Anti-Christ*, 1888, he declared "The Christian conception of God ... is one of the most corrupt conceptions of God on earth" (18). He became institutionalized shortly after. However, in *The Wanderer and the Shadow*, Nietzsche observes that "Morality without religion is impossible. Every purely moral system...ends in nihilism. One still hopes to go with a moralism without a religious background, but that necessarily leads to nihilism" (19). In *Human, All Too Human*, he professes his objections. I will list only two: A sage who calls upon us to no longer work, which is an obvious reference to Luther, whom I demonstrated he misunderstood; and secondly, the figure of the cross as a symbol in an age which no longer knows the meaning and shame of the cross. I suggest he was referring to the fact that the cross means to cross your nature (natural drives), as in *"Take up his cross daily and follow me,"* (*Lk.* 9:23), and intentionally suffer the supernatural path of self denial to become Ubermensch-the Superman. Moreover, as I said earlier, Nietzsche said the cross was primarily symbolic of Jesus bringing the kingdom of God to mankind now, not in the future, and despite the shame associated with His death, He harbored no resentment (*The Antichrist, 40*).

Santaniello tells us "It is no accident that the same person, that is, Nietzsche, who foretold the death in the belief of God, also was intelligent enough to foresee its consequences. And here are the results":

> If there is no belief in God, love and compassion have a propensity to evaporate.

If there is no belief in God, people become liable to inflict violence and cruelty on each other in an ever increasing scale and degree.

If there is no belief in God, human beings begin stockpiling weapons of global destruction that will slaughter their own children....

If there is no belief in God, human beings find no reason to refrain from violating and destroying everything.

If there is no belief in God, neither can conscience exist in its fullest form; the most diabolical and bestial in human beings takes over (201).

How far have we traveled from the golden rule, the categorical imperative espoused by Kant?! Only time will tell; well, it is telling us right now, and the light is dim, but maybe the closer we come to the magic year 2012, when the chakras begin their enhanced receptivity to cosmic forces-sun-moon-earth coordinates due to a rare galactic alignment that brings the solstice sun into alignment with the center of the Milky Way galaxy (Galactic Center), an event that occurs every 12,960 years, we will enjoy a greater understanding of the heart and soul of the pulse of the cosmos as it relates to us personally! The 2012 date is based on shamanic vision, city designs that mirror the cosmos above, and an awareness of precession aimed to calibrate a cosmic center in Mayan culture. Moreover, Egyptian wonders, esoteric astronomy within the tauroctony of the Mithras (origin of Mithraic Mysteries emerged from the precession/shifting of the vernal point), Vedic Yugas-Doctrine of the World of Ages, Islamic astronomy, symbolism of obelisks in France and esoteric astronomy encoded in Homer's *Iliad*, all suggest astronomical admonitions that alignments to the galaxy periodically occur, and that these alignments offer humans a chance for spiritual renewal. Even French alchemist Fulcanelli, in his interpretation of a monument in France, suggested the "end of time" signal provided by the Mayans. This end time is the end of darkness, materialism and illusion. In consideration of this galactic alignment theory, we have been falling deeper into unconsciousness for 12,960 years, and has as its shift zone between 1975-2021, when consciousness begins a reversal and gradual separation of spirit from the body consciousness-sleep, during each successive year. The pivotal year could be 2012 when the door to expanded perception is open the widest. According to this astronomical theory the door will close, meaning it is our duty to exploit this rare opportunity wherein the cosmic forces peak in their ability to pierce through our perineum (root chakra) charging our chakras maximally with its collected cosmic energy to cleanse and excite us with a burst of force that assists in developing our fullest spiritual potential.

I have spoken of the kabalistic internal inverted Tree of Life situated in man seemingly inimical to man's best interests; well, after all, why must our insides have feet that dangle in our head, or crown chakra, and our head rest down by our genitalia or root chakra? While I did speak about this anomaly earlier, choosing instead to save it for the closing comments, I did not mention that our inner Galactic Center is located in the center of the body, or at the root chakra, the seat of the latent evolutionary force and renewal of life; in other words, the Galactic Center is the root of this enigmatic cosmic tree! So powerful is our inner antennae called the spine, it is a receiving and emitting station that links us to every ounce of cosmological data. It is like a fractal that resembles the whole. This means we are profoundly prone to the consequences of its cosmic cycles such as: The Solstice sun's first contact and final clearance of the galactic equator: (1975-2021); The 2012 end-date of the Mayan 13-baktun cycle; The solstice sun's closest approach to the Galactic Center: 2220+/= three years. Year 2220 is also 2012 plus two Venus Round cycles of 104 years each (four Calendar Rounds); And year 6000 in the Jewish calendar, the dawn of the seventh shemittah: A.D. 2240.

Letters to a Skeptic

Because a primary point of soul's exit from the body is in the crown-head, it may be assumed that the Galactic Center should be in the head, as some say, but in consideration of the fact that Binah, or highest sephirah in the Inverted Tree of Life, is actually the root of this inverted system, we can conclude that the inner Galactic Center is adroitly located in the Root location. Regardless, both locations meld to one mystically anyway. An analogy can best explain this anomaly. Consider that plants undergo an inversion process once we consume them. In the plant's **effort** to spiritualize itself and transform its etheric root ball (plants, like animals and humans, have astral or etheric bodies while living and shortly after death) into a blossom of light, it inverts itself inside us so that the root ends up in the head or crown in its powerful striving for light. The head or Siva is the region of light reception in the body. It's as though the plant, in paying its dues karmically-cosmically for living in the darkness of the earth for so long, gets reprieve once it is eaten, that is, fulfills its destiny. I suggest that this very impetus for its powerful upward striving towards the Light, toward spiritualization, is predicated upon its life in darkness; and as a result, is not unlike the process humans undergo after a recognition that we, too, have been living so long in the darkness of the sensuous passions to the point of satiety, ad nauseam even, that we too, seek, with intensity, the upward reach towards the Light, toward Christ. This is the reason why Pythagoras required his students to eat plants or a vegetarian diet because in doing so he would be more assured his students could think clearly; he did not allow bean consumption however, because the essence of the digested-assimilated beans would migrate downward away from the head and bog down the digestive process, creating a heavy head-brain.

Just as this impending galactic event, due to calendrical shifts, affects our chakra system, so does it affect the uniqueness of cows, lions, birds, especially the eagle, and the butterfly to perform their destinies. The reason why the cow is so venerated by the Hindus is because her unique digestive system enables her (she eats one eighth of her weight daily-humans only one fortieth) to spiritualize earthen matter without her taking any spiritualized substance back upon death, unlike man, whom, in order to further transform his/her migration between lives, must harbor all the spiritualized substances he acquired during his earth life. During this prodigious eating process of the cow that binds her to earth matter, she is spiritualizing the earthen foodstuffs through her digestive process that is permeated with an astrality that reflects the entire cosmos, in turn, enabling her to create spiritual substances numerically necessary that are eventually emitted throughout space for man to accumulate in his legs and lower body in general. So vibrant and heavenly is her aura, her etheric body appears as the sun to the clairvoyant. Because she does not need this spiritualized substance after death, she leaves it earthbound for man to accumulate, and also for the earth so it can renew itself; this is why the Hindus consider the cow to be the true sacrificial creature, she gives but doesn't take back anything in return, unlike man and the eagle. The cow, unlike man and the eagle, is not a debtor to the earth, and is one of the reasons why the ancients, including Gurdjieff, consider man's debt to the earth so enormous that upon his sincere recognition of this, would cause enormous internal torment, hence his/her awakened newfound perception of the terror of the situation. The cow exemplifies the perfection of the measure-weight and number system, and as technology unknowingly tries to mimic what qualities are already perfected in the cow, the usefulness of the cow is reduced proportionally, and thereby, jeopardizing the cow's involvement in the measure-weight and number system needed to spiritualize the earth. The efficacy of the universe's ability to measure-weigh-number was assigned to the cow to distribute to mankind, something like all the technology needed for man's evolution is already found in the cow, and to tamper with her task, is to throw the otherwise masterful weight-measuring and numbering system inherent in the universe, i e. her servant the cow, off balance. Granted, this is a bizarre thought, but in the world of the occult that subscribes to the invisible world as the template and forerunner of external world phenomena and events, this idea is not far fetched, however unscientific it is. Finally, I'm not sure if he ever said this, but in the Gurdjieff system, the cow would represent the moving-instinctive brain, yet she epitomizes spiritualized forces, something like the aforementioned inverted Tree of Life and internalized plant anomalies.

I have mentioned the upward tending nature of plants inside the body, well, the upward tending nature of birds, especially the eagle, is also found to be a unique generator of spiritualized substances that belong to the head sphere, and corresponds to the nervous system in man. More than just feathered friends, these wondrous creatines are so prolific in their spiritualizing of heavenly substances for man to assimilate, that they appear as though they are not even of the earth. The eagle has preserved in his feathers the results of its interaction with Jupiter, the so called representative of the outer planets. The forces that emanate from the sun and find their way into the coordinated symbiotic efforts constructed by Jupiter, Mars, and Saturn, all culminate in the entire body and being of the eagle centered in the head, making the eagle a representative of the thinking part of man. Now the eagle steals his material substance from the earth, but allows it to be spiritualized by the forces spiritualized in the spirit world, and after death to his physical structure, he releases these spiritualized substances in the spirit world restoring balance: he stole from earth but gives back to the spirit world because he no longer needs the spiritualized substances he spiritualized from earthen matter for in his flight to this higher world he unites with the existing spiritualized substances of the spirit world. The eagle would represent the intellectual center in man in the Gurdjieff system, though I don't recall him ever saying this.

We've so far covered the crudeness of the cow, the lightness of the eagle, now we come to the ferocity of the lion, and ironically, it represents the feeling center in man. Fortunately for man and the earth, it is the lion that creates a balance between the spiritual and physical substances generated on earth *given* by the cow for the earth's and man's use, and those substances generated and *retained* by the eagle. This is so because the lion regulates his blood-circulation through the breathing, and in perfect balance relative to dynamic not quantity, all aided by his special affinity with the sun. Now the lion, unlike the eagle or cow who must work to acquire their physical and spiritual substances, the lion must simply breathe to acquire these substances, and as a result of this inherent balance between these substances, is able to regulate, upon death, perfectly through his group soul, how many eagles and cows are needed on the earth to maintain an equilibrium between spiritual and physical substance creation and distribution to assist evolution and involution for all creatures. The lion is representative of the sun animal due to its unique ability to absorb the potent forces of the sun. In fact, when the constellations above and below the sun are so aligned to exert the least influence upon the sun itself, the lion functions at its best. Now with the advent of the impending calendrical shift to occur, these processes may be either impeded or enhanced, but considering butterflies emanate spiritual substances while they are alive, though they too, are extremely amenable to planetary shifts, the efforts of the lion could very well be compensated for by these amazing heavenly flighty creatures.

    Humans are not unlike these four precious four animals. He too must absorb, assimilate and transform the hydrogen(s) contained within earth matter and spiritualize these materials to evolve and involve, except he is the only one that does so exclusively for himself and no other. But in consideration of the wondrous workings of the cosmos, what man cannot provide in the form of spiritualized substances for the spirit planes, the eagle provides, and what the eagle and man do not provide in the form of spiritualized earth substances, the cow provides, and to ensure a proper balance between the creation and distribution of these substances so essential for earthly and heavenly life, is provided by the lion and butterfly. However, unlike the bird, e.g., the eagle, whose bones are filled only with air, man's bones are filled with blood marrow, and it is here where the Christ Jesus mysteriously lives and breathes in and through us, just as the soul of the earth withdraws (inhales) into itself during the winter solstice, December 22, to accumulate the benefits culled from the sun drenched soil only to exhale once again during the summer solstice, or June 21, to replenish the earth with the properties it acquired during its rest in darkness. (The nature of the four animals was culled from Rudolf Steiner's Book, *Agriculture and Man*.)

Physicists and Number theorists repeatedly proclaim that science is not what people often think, and this is a point that Hume and Nietzsche made, namely, science is based on belief, and all that a scientist can do is demonstrate an idea that is less false! And as the physicists and number theorists say, the very beauty of science is enjoying the process of discovery, the very process of discovering new things, and even if they are proven wrong, the seed of joy is once again planted; the search once again for Beauty, the beauty of how things meld together, possibly spawned by an Anomaly in their respective field. What the physicists are saying is that, even amid the so-called scientific method of discovery that encompasses a methodological naturalism based on a data-driven study of nature, a certain belief and blind faith in the efficacy of what they are trying to accomplish is the motor that drives them onward. This is the same kind of faith that inspires the religious. Thank God for their Active Imagination(s) and its best friend faith; the world is a better place for those who seek a better understanding of what were previously supersensible subjects.

Celebrated natural philosopher (or scientist, as some would say), Francis Bacon, had this to say about the capacity to believe: "I had rather believe all the *fables* in the *Legend*, and the *Talmud*, and the *Alcoran*, then this universal frame is without a mind. And therefore God never wrought miracle to convince atheism, because his ordinary works convince it. It is true, that a little philosophy inclineth man's mind to atheism; but depth in philosophy bringeth men's mind to religion. For while the mind of man looketh upon second causes scattered, it may sometimes rest in them, and go no further; but when it beholdeth the chain of them, confederate and linked together, it must needs fly to Providence and Deity. Nay, even that school which is most accused of atheism doth most demonstrate religion; that is, the school of Leucippus and Democritus and Epicurus," (sp. 65 Francis Bacon, *The Essays*, Viscount St. Albans, ED.).

Keeping in mind Bacon's assertion, recall that I mentioned earlier that I would present a new finding relative to Darwin's Tree of Life that I know you would have a special interest in. I will not elaborate on this subject, but I will provide an excerpt from my *Salvo* journal:

> Scientists have recently unearthed all kinds of evidence that actually challenges common ancestry. The Cambrian explosion is as infamous within the scientific community as the "Darwin fish" is among Christians. In this ancient burst of life, which happened over 500 millions years ago, nearly all of the major living phyla (or basic body plans) of life appeared in a geological instant with no apparent evolutionary precursors. The Cambrian explosion even included vertebrate fish, which appeared without any hint of an evolutionary past. Even as Richard Dawkins concedes, "it is as though they were just planted there, without any evolutionary history." Perhaps this explains why Niles Eldredge, a prominent Darwinian paleontologist, acknowledged that "the higher up the Linnaean hierarchy you look, the fewer transitional forms there seem to be."

Letters to a Skeptic

Darwin's universal Tree of Life (TOL) is coming under assault not only from paleontology but also from genetic data. A recent Physorg.com article explains that a "minority of biologists and evolutionists have questioned the accuracy of the TOL hypothesis" even though similar genes exist in organism patterns that do not fit the universal "tree." As National Academy of Sciences (NAS) biologist W.F. Doolittle states, "evolutionary scientists will have failed to find the 'true tree,' not because their methods are inadequate, or because they have chosen the wrong genes, but because the history of life cannot properly be represented as a tree." Doolittle attributes this incapacity to gene-swapping among microorganisms at the base of the TOL. But another NAS member, Carl Woese, found that discrepancies between proposed evolutionary trees "can be seen everywhere in the universal tree, from its root to the major branchings within and among the various taxa to the makeup of the primary groupings themselves." This bears repeating. More than one NAS member is saying that modern genetic discoveries challenge Darwin's universal Tree of Life.

And other Darwinian biologists are concurring with Woese. "Despite the amount of data and breadth of taxa analyzed," writes biologist Sean B. Carroll, "relationships among most metazoan phyla remained unsolved." Carroll, who studies animal (metazoan) relationships at the University of Wisconsin, also explains that the "recurring discovery of persistently unresolved clades (bushes) should force a reevaluation of several widely held assumptions of molecular systematics." Unfortunately, one assumption Carroll does not reevaluate is that of common ancestry. Could it be that the inability to construct robust phylogenetic trees (evolutionary relationships) using genetic data simply indicates that common ancestry is wrong? (winter, '08, 13).

Ronne Gleason

To create a new nemesis in this entire evolutionary theory, Aaron Filler, a Harvard-trained evolutionary biologist and medical director at LA's Cedars-Sinai Institute for Spinal Disorders, says, "The other great apes we see now, such as chimps or gorillas or orangutans, might have descended from human-like ancestors." He based this finding on his analysis of over 250 living and extinct mammalian species, with some bones dating up to 220 million years old. Could we be in for another inversion, this time an inversion in Darwin's much prized Tree of Life?

Well, as Bacon says, there is a time when "second causes scattered... bring a man's mind to Providence or Deity." It appears that the longer the search goes on, the less sure scientists become of the theory of evolution. Meantime, the joy of discovery prods them on. They have a faith, some would say a fool's faith in light of contrary evidence, and whether the entire theory of evolution will be seen as a mere fable in centuries ahead remains to be seen, it was their search for what they imagined to be a connectedness of all things minus God that is meritorious; to them this was/is supernatural. Well my occult animal quadrivium serves the same purpose; that is, it helps us see a connection between seemingly disconnected entities, hopefully, a supernatural one. In either case however, a very Active Imagination nourished by intuitive energy is needed. Now how do these abstractions differ from a man's belief in God, possibly equally difficult to prove? even though St. Thomas Aquinas and Immanuel Kant have both proven, using pure logic, the existence of God. Ironically, pure logic cannot even prove evolution as mounting evidence is demonstrating. As I have stated in my last letter, God is to be seen as a God of Belief; this is the Islamic view; this is the Christian view. And while the very few scientists whom are atheists dangle their brains every which way knocking on this or that door of discovery, and whether God laughs, belches, or mourns over the entire pursuit, or whether the belly of the universe just gets

Letters to a Skeptic

fatter, it is not what you know that really matters, it is what you Believe! Active Imagination is a gift, and atheists, nihilists and empiricists are lacking this precious extension of their minds no lower animal can duplicate, not even the eagle, cow, lion or butterfly, all of whom function in exact accord with God's will since they do not have free will like man.

Finally, beginning this letter with a commentary on Active Imagination to set the tone for subsequent discussions about historical and mythical stories surrounding Jesus and Dionysos, I embellished my unannounced thesis (after all, this is only a letter, and I had no idea it would evolve into a fifty-eight page exploration) about the necessity for transcending empirical exegesis, and the psychological boundary imposed by non-metaphysical analysis, by demonstrating early on that if scientific giants such as Newton, Galileo and Kepler believed in the Christian God and its associated Orthodox Mysteries, how then can one who has less scientific understanding of the universe not believe that there exists something out there that is not comprehensible, God even, erewhile, realizing I was arguing my point with an empiricist, a person whose non-belief system has one key predicate: if it does not match my everyday experience, then it does not exist; therefore, is not believable, which is exactly why I knew it was futile to exploit persuasive inductive and deductive logic to make the inherently unreasonable reasonable. Moreover, using this same line of reasoning, I then illustrated that even renowned skeptic, David Hume, notable Christian satirist, Mark Twain, and proclaimed Antichrist, Friedrich Nietzsche, all accepted a monotheistic God, the former two especially later in life. I expounded at length on Nietzsche for this same reason; here we have a proclaimed antichrist, "God is dead" exponent, who so believed in God, in religion, that he devoted his entire life to finding ways to restore its original tenet, and however counter-poised, counter-positioning his efforts were, they always emanated from one central theme: the god-granted freedom to spiritualize the animal passions in order to feel the inner Jesus, the inner Buddha, the inner Dionysos/Ariadne! with an eye toward moving beyond himself by himself into the bottom-most depths of being like a seed down under, hoping to emerge from this subterranean darkness a new sprout that can trust God and His unfashionable ways, an ideal he probably culled from John: "Most assuredly, I say unto you, unless a grain of wheat falls into the ground and dies, it remains alone; but if it dies, it produces much grain" (*John* 12:24). By the way, this theme sums up the message of Dostoevsky's entire novel, *The Brothers Karamazov*, an author Nietzsche praised. Now, after revealing the consequences of the death of a belief in God from none other that the supposed antichrist, Friedrich Nietzsche, I unveil the cosmological Galactic Alignment theory and its relationship to man and his chakras. Finally, to really stretch the Active Imagination discussed early in this letter, I explore the possible symbiotic connection we have with the cow, eagle, lion and butterfly. I finally conclude with the thought that it appears that not even Darwin could outrun God, let alone aforementioned Newton, Galileo, Kepler, Hume, Twain or Nietzsche.

Thank you for being the priority that inspired this letter.

May The Universe Dance On Your Porch;
I Know I'm Dancing On Mine,

Ronne
3-4-2008

INDEX

Jacob Boehme 1
Hermes 1
Aesop's Fables 2
Adi Granth 2
Bhagavad Gita 2
Iliad 2
Odyssey 2
St. Augustine 2
Koran 2
Tolstory 3
Blaise Pascal 4
C.S. Lewis 5
Maupassant 5
Chesterton 5
Galileo 5
Isaac Newton 5
Jewish N Library 5
Dialogue 6
Johannes Kepler 6
Celestial Fire 7
George Gurdjieff 6
Calvin's Doctrine 6
Montaigne 7
Cicero 7
Karl Marx 8
Taoism 8
Hinduism 8
Sikhism 8
Buddhism 8
Islamism 8
Greek Proverbs 8
Dis-Identify 9
Plato 10
Aristotle 10

INDEX

Heidegger 10
Dasein 10
Plato's Sophist 10
The First Christian Histories 11
Tertullian 11
Bede's Ecclesiastical 11
John Sargent murals 11
Boston Public Library 11
Works of Josephus 13
Apollonius of Tyana 14
Christopher Marlowe 14
Cervantes 14
Bacon 14
Twain 14
Lost books of the Bible 14
Lost Gospel of Peter 14
The Pistis Sophia 15
Gnostic Gospel 15
Aquarian Gospel 16
Levi 17
Sacred School of Eliho & Salome 17
Book of Enoch 19
Melchizedek 20
Alexandria 20
Jesus & Ganid Friends 20
Error (evil) 22
Yahweh 23
Michael-Christ Story 24
Mithraic Teachings 25
Persian Mystery Cult 26
Constantine 26
St. Justin Martyr 26
St. Gregory 27
Jospeh Campbell 27
St. Basil 27
Homers' Odyssey 28

INDEX

Hesiod 28
Nietzsche 28
Carl Yung 29
Plato's Visions 29
Gnosticism 29
Spindle of Necessity 29
Pineal Gland 30
Pituitary Gland 30
Thyroid Gland 30
Thymus Gland 30
Adrenal Gland 30
Male & Female.. 30
Human Aura.. 30
Subtle Energies 30
Prana... 31
Fyodor Dostoevsky.. 32
Eastern Christian Orthodox....................................... 32
Silver Cord.. 32
Tree of Knowledge... 33
Plato's Doctrine of the Cross..................................... 35
Ante-Nicene Fathers 36
Protonica-wife of Claudius 36
Emperor Claudius 36
Moses 36
Protonica W. Claudius 36
Eusebius of Caesarea 37
Eternal Recurrence 37
Egyptian Ankh... 37
Nietzshe's uses & disadvantages History For Life.......... 38
Hume 39
Philo Dialogue 39
Cleanthes 39
The Bible & Twain 42
Dr. Rushmore.. 44
Twain & Religion 45

INDEX

Ulysses 45
John Milton Paradise 46
Leibniz 46
Eleazar 46
Lou Salome 47
Nietzshe's Christian Faith 47
Santaniello 48
Kantian Animals 48
God is Dead-Nietzsche 48
Schopenhaver 49
Plato & Christianity 49
David Strauss 50
Early Christianity 50
Birth of Tragedy 51
Martin Luther 51
Superman/Nietzsche 53
Fasting 55
Ascetic Method 56
Mephistophelian zeal 57
Assassins-Monks 60
Kant & Hegel 60
Nero-Roman Emperor 61
Dionysos 61
Petronius 61
Daniel 3 62
Athenagoras 63
Zeus 63
Persephone 63
Orpheus 64
Pythagoras 64
Hades 64
Bacchus's 65
Herodotus 66
Pindar 66
Thus Spake Zarathustra 67
Orphic Ascetic Teachings 68

INDEX

St. Francis of Assasi 68
R.C. Hogart 68
Orphic-Dion-initiation 68
Ariadne & Nietzsche 69
Homer 69
Carl Kerenyi 70
Sacred Marriage 70
Aphrodite 70
Law of Three 72
A Single Eye of Light 73
John Calvin 75
Reform Movement 75
Histories & Herodotus 76
Scythian's 76
Song of Solomon 78
Three Forms of Sexual Attraction 80
Artemis (goddess) 81
Zeus 81
Gospel of Philip 81
John Locke 83
Apophaticism 84
Vladimir Lossky 84
Doctrine of World of Ages 87
Galactic Center 87
Mayan 87
Kabalistic Internationalized 88
Pythagoras Vegetarian 89
Binah 89
Eagle 90
Gurdjieff-Man's debt 90
The Four precious animals—Rudolf Steiner 90
Hydrogen(s) 92
Richard Dawkins 94
Fables 94
Universal Tree of Life Challenged 95
Sean B. Carroll 95

INDEX

St. Thomas Aquinas 96
Galactic Alignment Theory...98

Bibliography of Works Cited in Brief
(These authors made my thesis possible)

Athanassakis, Apostolos, N. *Hesiod, Theogony, Works and Days, Shield*, Ins. 947-949. Bede, The Venerable. *Ecclesiastical Histories*
Dostoevsky, Fyodor. *House of the Dead, Notes From the Underground, Crime and Punishment, The Injured and Insulted, The Brothers Karamazov.*
Euripides. Bacchae, p.194
Galileo. *Dialogues on the Two Great World Systems.*
Goethe, Wolfgang. *Faust.*
Harvey, George. *Harper Magazine*, Ed.
Heidegger, Martin. *Plato's Sophist.*
Harrison, Thomas. *Divinity and History*, p. 217.
Herodotus, *Histories*, Oxford World Classics.
Bogart, R.C. *The Hymns of Orpheus.*
Hume, David. *Natural History of Religion, Dialogues, In My Own Life.*
Kerenyi, Carl. *Dionysos, Archetypical Images of Indestructible Life*, p. 112.
Josephus, Flavius. *The Works of Josephus.*
Levi. *The Aquarian Gospel of Jesus The Christ.*
Locke, John. *The Reasonableness of Christianity.*
Lossky, Vladimir. *Mystical Theology of the Eastern Church*, p. 42.
Luther, Martin. *Basic Theological Writings*, p. 157, *Selections From His Writings*, pgs. 67, 68.
Milton, John. *Paradise Lost.*
Nietzsche, Friedrich Wilhelm. *Journal Notes*, vol. 7, pgs. 30, 32, 34, 70, 72, 77, *Day Break*, pgs. 560, 113. *Twilight of the Idols*, p. 109, *The Wanderer and His Shadow*, p. 65, *Thus Spake Zarathustra, The Anti-Christ*, p. 20, 40, 42, *The Gay Science*, p. 125, sect. 343, *In Human, All Too Human, The Birth*

of Tragedy, On the Genealogy of Morals, pgs. 115,120,121, 148, 150, 151. *Beyond Good and Evil*, p.160, 203, 21.
Petronius. *Satyricon.*
Plato. *Collected Dialogues, Including the Letters*, ed. by Edith Hamilton and Huntington Cairms, Bollingen Series LXXI-Princeton.
Santaniello. *Nietzsche and the Gods*, p. 159, 164.
Schaff, Phillip. *History of the Christian Church*, pgs. 11-17.
Schepps, Solomon, J., Foreword and Trans. *The Lost Books of the Bible.*
Steiner, Rudolph. *Agriculture and Man.*
Strauss, David. *David Strauss, The Confessor and the Writer.*
Tolstoy, Leo. *The Spiritual Writings*, p. 176
Twain, Mark *Captain Stormfield 's Visit to Heaven, The Bible According to Twain, Concerning the Character of the Real God.*
Wahrer, Harry Scott Prepared and executed *The Melchizedek Bible*, published by The Embassy of The Dominion of Melchizedek.
Yung, Carl. *Symbols of Transformation*, pgs. 26-29.

About the Author

Prior to earning his master's and doctoral degrees in Theology, Ronne Gleason earned his bachelor's degree from the University of Michigan with concentrations in psychology and philosophy. For three years he did post graduate work in world religions and foreign literature at Harvard University. He graduated from Cornell University's School of Industrial and Labor Relations Human Resources Studies Program. He earned a Doctoral degree in Naturopathy from the Trinity College of Natural Health, with his dissertation addressing alternative therapies for Autism. Ronne Gleason has authored two books, titled, *A Single Eye of Light: Sacred Visions (Poems and Letters)*, and also, *Moments at Anchor Bay High (Souls on Fire)*.

Gleason has lived in lower Michigan for seventy-five years, forty four of those years on the picturesque Salt River, and with his brother since 2017 where they both enjoy kayaking.